GOD OUR
TEACHER

Other Books by Robert W. Pazmiño

Basics of Teaching for Christians
By What Authority Do We Teach?
Foundational Issues in Christian Education (2d ed.)
Latin American Journey
Principles and Practices of Christian Education
The Seminary in the City

GOD OUR TEACHER

Theological Basics in Christian Education

Robert W. Pazmiño

Baker Academic
A Division of Baker Book House Co
Grand Rapids, Michigan 49516

Published by Baker Academic
a division of Baker Book House Company
P.O. Box 6287, Grand Rapids, MI 49516-6287

Printed in the United States of America

Library of Congress Cataloging-in-Publication Data

Pazmiño, Robert W., 1948–
    God our teacher : theological basics in Christian education /
Robert W. Pazmiño
      p.   cm.
    Includes bibliographical references and index.
    ISBN 0-8010-2284-3 (pbk.)
      1. Christian education—Philosophy. 2. Theology, Doctrinal.
I. Title
    BV1464 .P3792   2002
    268'.01—dc21   2001037316

For information about academic books, resources for Christian leaders, and all new releases available from Baker Book House, visit our web site:
http://www.bakerbooks.com

Dedicated to Wanda Ruth Pazmiño,
my wife and life companion

CONTENTS

INTRODUCTION

Ultimately, life and theology come down to God and us. Therefore, the ultimate questions about life can be viewed in terms of our relationships with others and our communion with God. For Christians, the essential relationship of life is that between God and us. In this relationship, God serves as the ultimate teacher, our teacher throughout eternity. An interest in God as teacher is re-emerging in discussions of education. In a chapter from his recent work titled *God's Wisdom*, Peter Hodgson insightfully traces the history of theological thought on this theme.[1]

The Christian faith claims that God is most wonderfully revealed in Jesus Christ and in the continuing revelation of the Holy Spirit. Therefore, God's revelation is the starting point for our learning. We begin in chapter 1 with a discussion of the core distinctive of Christianity—the Trinity. The Trinity discloses a communion as God the Father, Son, and Spirit reveal for humanity and all of creation the essence of life in its fullness. A further claim advanced in this work is that the Trinity is an organizing theological theme for the theory and practice of Christian education. The vitality of Christian education depends on the theological roots of the Trinity. These roots require thoughtful consideration and application to teaching practice.

The importance of knowing God as teacher finds warrant from a surprising source. Job's friend Elihu poses the basic question for Job and all of us: "Who is a teacher like him?" (Job 36:22). The implication is that there is no teacher like God the

Father, Son, and Spirit. They have taught humanity since time began. So the biblical record affirms the Triune God as our ultimate teacher.

The relationship between God and us is explored in the following pages through six terms of relationality or communion that serve as connectors for each chapter. These six prepositions—*for*, *despite*, *with*, *in*, *through*, and *beyond*—provide the terms to wrestle with the implications our communion with God has for the relational ministry of Christian education. Prepositions serve to address the vital connection between God and humanity, between God and all of creation. They serve to partially disclose the grammar of relationality inherent in creation. Emphasizing relationship is appropriate in the light of the centrality of the Trinity in Christian faith and the place of covenant in Scripture. Covenant sets the terms of our relationship with God. Each of the six relational terms also provides a connection between Christian theology and the ministry of teaching. Each term provides an entry point into traditional theological loci: the Trinity, sin and salvation, Jesus Christ as incarnation, the Holy Spirit, the Christian church, and the consummation.[2] In more formal theological categories, the six chapters explore aspects of theology proper, harmartiology and soteriology, Christology, pneumatology, ecclesiology and missiology, and eschatology.

For each chapter's theological explorations, I assume the perspective of a practical theologian focusing on Christian education, a perspective I trust will offer insights for the crucial ministry of teaching in the third millennium. Without attention to Christian education from a theologically informed perspective, the Christian church is subject to cultural isolation and eventual extinction. That alternative fails to be faithful to the call to love God with all of our minds. As teachers of the Christian faith, we need our minds to be theologically informed, formed, and transformed. A lesser commitment fails to give glory to the God who desires to be our teacher in this life and in the life to come.

Writing about God as teacher is an audacious task that calls for humility. In reviewing the original outline for this work, Julie Gorman shared two insightful suggestions. She suggested adding chapters on God *above* us and God *through* us. In light of her response, I renamed chapter 5 "God *Through* Us" instead of my earlier thought of "God *Among* Us." *Through* suggests a more active focus on ministry and mission in the church. Julie's suggestion of God *above* us is, I hope, a spirit embraced in all the chapters of this work. The human art of speaking and writing about God is presumptuous and fraught with danger. Nevertheless, a faith stance struggles for understanding, recognizing that God is ever and always above, below, and all about us. This is what the Apostle Paul shared with his audience in Athens:

> The God who made the world and everything in it, he who is Lord of heaven and earth, does not live in shrines made by human hands, nor is he served by human hands, as though he needed anything, since he himself gives to all mortals life and breath and all things. From one ancestor he made all nations to inhabit the whole earth, and he allotted the times of their existence and the boundaries of the places where they would live, so that they would search for God and perhaps grope for him and find him—though indeed he is not far from each one of us. For "In him we live and move and have our being"; as even some of your own poets have said. (Acts 17:24–28)

In God we live, move, and have our being. Any attempt to write about God must recognize God's mystery, being above us as wholly other and transcendent. This faith stance honors God's sovereignty and offers insights that require further dialogue and response. I share this in the spirit of recognizing God above us, yet wonderfully revealed in Jesus Christ as Paul shared with his Greek audience: "While God has overlooked the times of human ignorance, now he commands all people everywhere to repent, because he has fixed a day on which he will have the world judged in righteousness by a man whom he has appointed, and of this he has given assurance to all by raising him from the dead" (Acts 17:30–31). The incarnation and resurrection of Jesus Christ bear witness to God's active teaching of humanity leading to the consummation of creation.

Though several of my previous works considered the theological basics in Christian education, this book makes that task explicit. It gathers up insights from my earlier works and explores new ground. It proposes that theological basics provide the constitutive framework for teaching practices. In particular, I suggest that the Trinity provides a theological ordering that enables those who teach to imaginatively engage their ministry. The shared life *(perichoresis)* of the Trinity invites those called to teach to embrace the mystery of living in the world with a vision of God's future. Teaching, like other practices of the Christian church, requires celebrating the already of God's fulfilled purposes while awaiting the not yet. The dynamic life of the already and not yet finds expression in the teaching ministry of Jesus, which is the topic of chapter 3. The heart of this work resides in the third chapter where teaching is incarnated in Jesus' exemplary ministry.

In my earlier works, most explicitly in *Principles and Practices of Christian Education*, I identified two underlying forms and two organizing principles for Christian education. The two forms are the educational trinity of content, persons, and context, and the five-task model of proclamation, community formation, service, advocacy, and worship. The two principles are those of conversion or transformation and connection.[3] In this work, a third form and third principle emerge from my theological considerations, which, when related to my earlier writings, serve to introduce the underlying structure and theological passion for what follows.

In relation to forms, my idea of an educational trinity affirms a rootedness in divine trinitarian life with a corresponding concern for orthodoxy in educational thought. My identification of a five-task model of proclamation, community formation, service, advocacy, and worship affirms the dynamic of the church's mission in the world and a concern for orthopraxis in educational practice. My introduction of a third Chalcedonian form affirms both the order and ardor or passion of relationships between our primary identity in huddling with God (differentiation and particularity) and our mission of mixing in the world as God's people (unity and universality). Chalcedonian form in education embraces the concern for *orthopathos* in theology introduced by theologian Samuel Solivan. Orthopathos is right and true passion that connects orthodoxy as right and true belief with orthopraxis as right and just action.[4] Orthopathos maintains the distinctions and tensions in relationships, but sets clear priorities of the heart, mind, and will. Orthopathos is guided by the order of loves that Jesus identified in the two great commandments for humanity—loving God and loving our neighbors as ourselves.

In relation to principles, the principle of conversion affirms the place of transformation in education that Christians claim is possible through God's gracious work in the person of the Holy Spirit. The principle of conversion emerges from the biblical covenant of redemption in Jesus Christ. The principle of connection affirms the interdependent web of relationships that flows from an ecological consciousness of our human and created situation. The principle of connection emerges from the covenant of creation. The Galilean principle introduced in chapter 3 affirms our huddling with God and God's people to form a clear sense of identity complemented by our mixing with the diversity of humanity. Huddling embraces particularity while mixing embraces universality. Huddling embraces differentiation while mixing embraces unity. Both are exemplified in the teaching ministry of Jesus the Galilean.

Both the Chalcedonian form and the Galilean principle discussed in chapter 3 emerge from considering in-depth the human life and teaching ministry of Jesus Christ. "Bernard Ramm has observed that without Jesus Christ we cannot comprehend our own humanity."[5] A Christian understanding of education can be had only by revisiting the life, teaching ministry, and theological significance of Jesus the Master Teacher.

This work offers one perspective that invites further discussion of the essential theological basics to guide the theory and practice of Christian education. My personal theological perspective has been identified as being that of an ecumenical evangelical Christian, and I speak as a North American Hispanic person. Any labeling of my stance will, I hope, provide bridges for a wider dialogue across both Christian and religious traditions different from my own. This invitation is implicit in an understanding of the Trinity that honors God's plenitude, God's grace as revealed in all of creation that can include other religious traditions.[6] The affirmation of general revelation and common grace does not discount the distinctive Christian claims of special revelation and grace in Jesus Christ or the unique salvation offered in communion with the Triune God. Teaching provides the occasion to identify, celebrate, and share the distinctives of a religious tradition. I pray that this work will contribute toward that end as I celebrate the connections between Christian theology and education.

A concern for theological basics or essentials persists throughout this work. Each chapter concludes with an essential teaching that offers a connection between theology and Christian education. The essential teaching of this introduction is the following: God is our teacher for this time and all times to come.

I wish to acknowledge the wise counsel of colleagues who responded to my first draft of this work. Kevin Lawson, Eileen Starr, and Dana Wright diligently provided comments that helped to clarify my thoughts. I have not always followed their advice, so I must assume responsibility for any gaps in this work. The choices I have made reflect my theology of Christian education that is still in process until the consummation.

ONE

GOD FOR US: THE TRINITY AND TEACHING

The Trinity is the great mystery of the Christian faith that believers over the centuries have sought to understand and share with others through their teaching. The idea of one God revealed in three persons has stretched the human imagination and has been a source of strength and wonder. Teaching this core doctrine of the faith has been a challenge in each age as Christians seek to proclaim the truth in ways that affect everyday life. The purpose of this first chapter is to revisit this precious Christian truth with a particular interest in making connections to the ministries of teaching. James Smart, in his now classic work *The Teaching Ministry of the Church*, suggested that the doctrine of the Trinity is the essential starting point for understanding the theological bases of Christian education.[1] The Trinity is the place to start in understanding how God is *for* us as well as *despite, with, in, through,* and *beyond* us.

In recent years theologians have reconsidered the doctrine or teaching of the Trinity. This is appropriate since each generation of Christians has the responsibility, indeed the divine calling, to express its understanding of God in ways that address its distinctive setting and audience. In this effort, Christians cannot ignore the thoughts of those who came before them in the advance of the church. Christians have the obligation of dis-

15

cerning points of continuity with historical formulations of the faith and of struggling with new light and truth as it breaks forth from various sources. While this is a precarious task, refusing to engage it relegates the Christian gospel to a secondary place in the affairs of human life. The Christian faith claims God's revelation discloses reality that humanity ignores at the expense of experiencing life at its fullest.

To engage the theological task of understanding and teaching about the Trinity requires openness to the ongoing ministry of the Holy Spirit. The Holy Spirit is the promised tutor who assists Christians in wrestling with God's truths and sharing their discoveries with others. Jesus promised to send the Spirit of truth to his followers in their ongoing ministry of making disciples and teaching them all that Jesus himself taught (John 14:26; 15:26; 16:7; Matt. 28:18–20). The Spirit of Christ discloses to Jesus' followers those truths they need to live and to nurture the faith of rising generations.

I approach this work of recovering an understanding of the Trinity from the perspective of a practical theologian with a particular commitment to Christian education. I draw upon the research and writings of other theologians who have an interest in classical, systematic, and biblical theology with the hope of gaining new insight and wisdom for the task of teaching the Christian faith in a postmodern world.[2] This inquiry presumes an understanding of the Trinity from a faith perspective that affirms this core Christian belief as essential. In fact, the Trinity serves as an organizing grammar and theme for Christian education in all of its dimensions. While this thought is not new in the history of the Christian church, the application to current educational thought and practice may provide some additional insights for those engaged in and concerned for effective Christian education in the third millennium.[3]

My interest in the implications of our understanding of and experience with the blessed Trinity for teaching derives from the work of Nels Ferré, a systematic theologian who worked with D. Campbell Wyckoff, a renowned Christian educator. In his work *A Theology for Christian Education*, Ferré proposed a trinitarian model with God the Father as the educator, Jesus Christ the Son as the exemplar, and the Holy Spirit as the tutor.[4] My fascination with how the life and activity of the Trinity impacts all areas of human and created life naturally leads me to consider the areas of practical theology and Christian ministry. Practical theology, according to Karl Barth, deals with the question of "how the Word of God may be served by human words" and actions, including the words and actions of teachers.[5] Christian ministry, specifically Christian education and teaching, occupies my professional life. In addition, my reading of two recent works from quite different authors convinced me of the importance of making the explicit connection between the Trinity and teaching in a work that explores theological basics for Christian education.

Two Recent Works

The first work was that of Peter Toon, an Anglican theologian who has taught theology in England, the United States, and abroad for about thirty years. Toon is the president of the Prayer Book Society of the Episcopal Church. Being baptized at birth in an Episcopal church, but later raised as a Baptist and again baptized as an adult, I was delighted to return to my ecclesiastical roots through Toon's writing. His work *Our Triune God: A Biblical Portrayal of the Trinity* skillfully explores the depths of the biblical record for the existence and priority of a trinitarian pattern. He effectively defends the essential role of the Trinity in Christian belief, faith, and practice.[6] Toon's work affirmed the continuing importance of returning to our Christian roots to gain perspective and remain faithful to the gospel delivered to us. I am reminded of a proverb from Jewish spiritual educator Abraham Heschel. Heschel noted that "thinking without roots will bear flowers but no fruit."[7] Being raised in a predominantly Jewish neighborhood in Brooklyn, New York, I found Heschel's insights to ring true. Returning to the roots of the Christian faith as discovered in the Scriptures is essential for any Christian who desires to teach the faith. The scriptural roots affirm the Trinity as a core Christian belief that is essential and nonnegotiable.

The second work that I encountered was *Renewing America's Soul: A Spiritual Psychology for Home, Work, and Nation* by Howard E.

Butt, Jr.[8] Butt is the president of the H. E. Butt Foundation and the Laity Lodge Retreat Center in Kerrville, Texas. A business-man for fifty years, he has been active as a lay leader seeking to bridge the secular and religious worlds. In his book, Butt sees the Triune God as the organizing theme underlying all of life, includ-ing the "common fabric of daily life."[9] Just as Toon argues for the importance of the Trinity for Christian faith, Butt argues for the importance of the Trinity for life in a variety of spheres including the home, work, and nation. Drawing upon his understanding of psychology and the Scriptures, he presents a convincing exam-ple of how trinitarian thinking can be generative for creative min-istry and life faithful to the gospel of Jesus Christ.

After reading these two works, the challenge posed for me as a Christian educator was to consider teaching in relation to the Trin-ity. This chapter will first survey recent scholarship that addresses the Trinity, going beyond the works of Toon and Butt to consider others like Catherine LaCugna and Leonardo Boff. Recent schol-arship affirms the historic orthodox belief in the Triune God that has served to distinguish the Christian faith from other faiths. In light of this affirmation, I suggest that the Trinity serves as an orga-nizing theme for the thought and practice of Christian education.

The last section of the chapter considers how trinitarian think-ing influences educational questions. My hope is that this prac-tical theological exploration will serve to foster the connection of faith to life. In a time of societal fragmentation, a search for meaning in all areas of life calls for a grounding that can sustain us. I believe that this grounding can be found in God revealed in three persons—the Triune God in whom we live, move, and have our being (Acts 17:28).

The Trinity in Recent Scholarship

The title for this chapter was suggested to me by the provoca-tive work of Catherine LaCugna entitled *God for Us*.[10] In this work, LaCugna revisits the doctrine of the Trinity with a focus upon the relationships that exist among the persons of the Trin-ity and between divinity and humanity. Her thesis is, "The doc-trine of the Trinity is ultimately a practical doctrine with radical consequences for the Christian life."[11] LaCugna addresses the separation between trinitarian doctrine and Christian life by exploring soteriology, the understanding of salvation.[12] She insightfully relates our understanding of the Trinity to God's works of salvation that demonstrate God's care and love. God's care and love provide the foundation for human caring expressed through teaching ministries. However, it is important to note that the focus needs to be upon salvation *for* more than salvation *from*. Salvation *from* sin and various forms of oppression is not to be devalued in any way. Rather, a focus upon salvation *for* implies the need for clarity regarding the purposes of education. My five-task model of proclamation, community formation, service, advocacy, and worship is just one attempt to identify these perennial purposes. How do these purposes connect to Christian education?[13] We must ask ourselves, what do we educate *for*? In other words, why should we educate? To what ends do we teach? We educate for God, for others, for ourselves. We also educate for certain outcomes and competencies. But we can lose perspective if these measures are not related to the wider purposes of God and of all humanity. For example, in the press for unity in education, we may not honor the diversity that exists. However, we must also recognize the dangers of unending plurality that fails to affirm an essential unity. In this, the Trinity provides a model for us. Diversity exists in the Trinity, but it is a diversity of three. This is not an unending plurality. In addition, with the three also exists the one God in a unity of purpose and life that models the possibility of partnership, relationship, and mutuality that humanity desires.

The relationships revealed to humanity in the Trinity provide the model for the relationships that can be nurtured through Christian education. Education is clearly not equated with the salvation offered to humanity in the person and work of Jesus Christ. However, Christian education can be a vehicle in the process of salvation that God elects to use to increase the faith, hope, and love of persons. Richard Osmer makes this connection in his recent proposal that Christian education must focus on education for faith, hope, and love related respectively to the perennial teaching tasks of catechesis, discernment, and edification.[14] Historically, Richard Baxter (1615–91), a seventeenth-century

Puritan pastor, affirmed this insight in his autobiography when he observed, "I afterward perceived that education is God's ordinary way for the conveyance of his grace, and ought no more to be set in opposition to the Spirit than the preaching of the Word."[15]

The Christian teaching that God is for humanity, that God is for us and all of creation, provides the foundation and context for teaching the Christian faith. Because God is for us, we risk being for others in our teaching, supporting them with truth that is shared and explored together. Because God is for us, we dare to speak the truth in love and confront the patterns of death and destruction that result from sin. Because God is for us, we provide the time and space where persons can be receptive to God's demands and callings. Because God is for us, we share the sources for healing the human mind, body, and spirit and for ministries of reconciliation. Because God is for us, we imagine with hope a new day that embraces the *shalom* God intends for all believers and all of creation. Because God is for us, we risk the foolishness of teaching, expecting God's Spirit to work in human hearts and minds. Because God is for us, we celebrate the beauty that God has blessed upon persons, and we lament the daily suffering that visits many lives. Because God is for us, we pray for students, teachers, and all those related to teaching ministries with the expectation that God can teach us all if we have ears to hear and hearts and minds that are receptive. Karl Barth captured the significance of the God of the gospel being *for* us in the following words:

> By definition, the God of Schleiermacher cannot show mercy. The God of the Gospel can and does. Just as his oneness consists in the unity of his life as Father, Son, and Holy Spirit, so in relation to the reality distinct from him he is free *de jure* and *de facto* to be the God of *man*. He exists neither *next* to man nor merely *above* him, but rather *with* him, *by* him and most important of all, *for* him. He is *man's* God not only as Lord but also as father, brother, friend; and this relationship implies neither a diminution nor in any way a denial, but, instead a confirmation and display of his divine essence itself.[16]

Barth's words provide grounding for what LaCugna later emphasizes in God being *for* us.

In addition to LaCugna's work, Leonardo Boff, in his work titled *Trinity and Society*, contributes to an understanding of the persons of the Trinity. He proposes that a person be defined as "a *being-for* . . . an identity formed and completed on the basis of relationships with others."[17] Teaching requires an understanding of persons who are present and participating. Christian teaching requires a theological anthropology in terms of relationships. Persons as *beings-for* suggest the need to consider the purposes, directions, commitments, and ministries of participants. The concern for human freedom in education includes a consideration of a freedom *for* beyond the freedom *from* any sources of oppression. Freedom *for* requires consideration of God's purposes and God's demands in relation to human callings and vocations. God's purposes are essential to human fulfillment, and God's demands often stand in contrast to human needs as defined autonomously by persons. Relationships with others and particularly with God are constitutive of the human community as it seeks to reflect the divine community of the Trinity. Persons created in God's image find their highest fulfillment in reflecting this reality. Boff's work has been helpful in reappropriating an understanding of *perichoresis* or the mutual communion of the Trinity. Each person of the Trinity is a being for others. Therefore, the tasks of Christian education include the formation and transformation of persons as beings for others. This being for others does not discount the care of self that is a particular challenge for females in some cultures, but affirms the care of self as the complement to the care of others.[18] A Christian community is called to foster relationships of mutual care and nurture. Recognition of being created in God's image implies a sense of mystery in life and an openness to life-in-community. True freedom is found in fulfilling God's purposes for life that is shared in community with God and others. It is not good that persons be alone (Gen. 1:27; 2:18).

Beyond LaCugna and Boff's works, a number of theologians have revisited the Trinity in recent scholarship. This effort reflects the current need to identify Christian distinctives in an age of religious pluralism. What distinguishes Christian faith from the other monotheistic faiths of Judaism and Islam? What can Christians offer in their teaching to persons hungering for spiritual vitality and reality in a global postmodern culture? What difference can the Trinity make among members of Generation X and Generation Y who value relationships and community? How can spiritual resources make a difference in everyday life and provide perspective for navigating through a media culture? Why bother with a mystery of God being one in three and three in one? Theological scholarship has offered hope and perspective while delineating a distinctive Christian identity.

Drawing upon contemporary scholarship, Gabriel Fackre provides a helpful summary of a theological understanding of the Trinity:

> God is triune—three co-eternal, co-equal Persons in one Being. This ancient formula that seems so abstract to our pragmatic American minds is integral to the Christian story. It tells us *what* God wills is grounded in *who* God is. God is a trinitarian Life Together, and wills that way for the world. The mutuality and equality in deity are not only the ground and goal of the unfolding biblical drama, but also the model for human relationships in both church and society. The *diakonia* of the church in its mission to the world and the *koinonia* of the Christian community rise out of the *kerygma* that proclaims the unity and partnership of the triune God. So *didache* as introduction to the Trinity (as well as *leitourgia* as the nourishment of trinitarian praise) can interrelate the dimensions of the church's life and witness and contribute to the contextualizing of faith.[19]

Fackre's insights suggest the importance of attending to who God is as a basis for understanding the persons encountered in teaching. The life together in educational encounters should ideally reflect the qualities of the life together revealed in the Trinity. Attention to what God wills for humanity and all of creation flows from who God is. Fackre notes the mutuality and equality in God as providing a model for educational relationships. The unity and partnership of the Triune God are also suggestive for educational purposes. Fackre's broader emphasis upon the dimensions of the Christian story is provocative for Christian education that emerges at the intersection of the Christian story with both personal and communal stories. His words connect Christian education with the tasks of the church, including *kerygma, koinonia, diakonia, didache,* and *leitourgia.* My formulation of these tasks identifies *propheteia* or advocacy as an additional task, with *didache* involving the connective linkage across the five tasks rather than a separate task of the church. He suggests that *didache* or teaching serves as an introduction to the Trinity. This I can affirm with the expansion of such an introduction to include a holistic response that engages intellectual, affective, intentional, and behavioral dimensions and influences personal and corporate life.

An Old Testament Encounter

Recent scholarship serves to expand upon an orthodox core for understanding the Trinity as God revealed to humanity in the Scriptures. A passage from the Old or First Testament that relates to my dominant metaphor for teaching is found in Genesis 18:1–15, an account of the Lord's appearance to Abraham and Sarah by the oaks of Mamre:

> The LORD appeared to Abraham by the oaks of Mamre, as he sat at the entrance of his tent in the heat of the day. He looked up and saw three men standing near him. When he saw them, he ran from the tent entrance to meet them, and bowed down to the ground. He said, "My lord, if I find favor with you, do not pass by your servant. Let a little water be brought, and wash your feet, and rest yourselves under the tree. Let me bring a little bread, that you may refresh yourselves, and after that you may pass on—since you have come to your servant." So they said, "Do as you have said." And Abraham hastened into the tent to Sarah, and said, "Make ready quickly three measures of choice flour, knead it, and make cakes." Abraham ran to the herd, and took a calf, tender and good, and gave it to the servant, who hastened to prepare it. Then he took curds and milk and the calf that he had prepared, and set it before them; and he stood by them under the tree while they ate.
>
> They said to him, "Where is your wife Sarah?" And he said, "There, in the tent." Then one said, "I will surely return to you in due season, and your wife Sarah shall have a son." And Sarah was listening at the tent entrance behind him. Now Abraham and Sarah were old, advanced in age; it had ceased to be with

Sarah after the manner of women. So Sarah laughed to herself, saying, "After I have grown old, and my husband is old, shall I have pleasure?" The LORD said to Abraham, "Why did Sarah laugh, and say, 'Shall I indeed bear a child, now that I am old?' Is anything too wonderful for the LORD? At the set time I will return to you, in due season, and Sarah shall have a son." But Sarah denied, saying, "I did not laugh"; for she was afraid. He said, "Oh yes, you did laugh."

This passage recounts an extraordinary encounter with God's messengers or perhaps even with God himself. Abraham and Sarah hasten to prepare a meal for the three unexpected guests at the entrance to their tent. The visitors promise a son to Abraham and Sarah. Their reaction is understandably one of disbelief and laughter at the prospect of bearing a child in their old age. The visitor addressed as "lord" poses the provocative and lingering question for Sarah and Abraham in verse 14, "Is anything too wonderful for the LORD?" The question is one that persists for believers and those who teach the Christian faith.

Commentators on this passage have wondered who these dinner guests were. In interpreting such passages, Christian commentators can consider the insight of Karl Barth: "The New Testament is concealed within the Old, and the Old Testament is revealed by the New."[20] Peter Toon comments on the history of interpreting this passage. Patristic theological interpretation involved a trinitarian orientation and some believed that "here and there God actually revealed himself (howbeit in an indirect manner) to be Three in One and One in Three."[21] Toon cites the late William G. T. Shedd's edition of Augustine's classic study *De Trinitate*:

> The theophanies of the Pentateuch are trinitarian in their implication. They involve distinctions in God—God sending, and God sent; God speaking of God, and God speaking to God. The trinitarianism of the Old Testament has been lost to some in the modern [i.e., late 19th century] construction of the doctrine. The patristic, medieval and reformation theologies worked this vein with thoroughness, and the analysis of Augustine in this respect is worthy of careful study.[22]

Toon points out that "in the modern era (i.e., late twentieth century) the trinitarianism of the Old Testament has been lost sight of to an even greater degree than in 1887 when Shedd wrote these words. The sole use of the historical-critical method serves to hide the Holy Trinity from view."[23] Toon points out that Augustine's trinitarian interpretation of Genesis 18 indicates that "the interchange of the singular and plural references is most striking and intriguing."[24] Toon notes that the trinitarian interpretation of this incident is "most beautifully presented in pictorial form by the late fourteenth or early fifteenth-century icon by Andrej Rublev, *The Holy Trinity*, which is in the Tretyakov Gallery, Moscow."[25] In his portrayal, Rublev drew upon a long exegetical and iconographic tradition. He painted the Trinity that he, as a Christian, saw as coming to dinner. In his icon, three angels are at a table on which were served bread and wine. The Three Persons of God are at one table and their communion (*perichoresis*) is represented by the one loaf of bread and the one cup.[26] These elements are suggestive of the meal Jesus later initiated with his disciples. Other Christian commentators propose the dinner guests to be a preincarnate visit of the Second Person of the Trinity, the Word of God later revealed as Jesus of Nazareth, along with two angels. However one settles the question, this passage from Genesis 18 describes an amazing and playful encounter with God, bringing surprise and even laughter to Sarah and Abraham. It suggests a sense of mystery in dealing with God's visitation to humanity.

Recalling Barth's insight about interpretation, Christians can affirm two lessons from this passage. First, God is revealed as three with a mystery associated with the plural and singular divine realities. Though only implied in this Genesis passage, Christians name this reality "Trinity." Second, God amazingly seeks out an encounter with persons. The very God of the universe, suggestively revealed as three, desires a relationship that reflects the common life shared by the Father, Son, and Holy Spirit.

What might this passage suggest regarding Christian education? One image that I write about in my work *Basics of Teaching for Christians* is putting a feast on the table.[27] Another Old

Testament passage that makes this image explicit is Proverbs 9:1–6 where wisdom's feast is described:

> Wisdom has built her house, she has hewn her seven pillars. She has slaughtered her animals, she has mixed her wine, she has also set her table. She has sent out her servant-girls, she calls from the highest places in the town, "You that are simple, turn in here!" To those without sense she says, "Come, eat of my bread and drink of the wine I have mixed. Lay aside immaturity, and live, and walk in the way of insight."

Teaching is like artfully setting an inviting table that welcomes all to participate and can result in joyful celebration. The astounding suggestion from Abraham and Sarah's encounter by the oaks of Mamre is that God in the persons of the Trinity seeks table fellowship with humanity. As Sarah and Abraham prepared a table for their dinner guests that parallels the preparation made for teaching, so God's presence at the table brings the promise of new life. For Abraham and Sarah, this new life was represented in the birth of a son when they were old. The manifestations of new life will vary with the circumstances of each person at the table, but the invitation in Christian education is to learn of and encounter the Living God revealed in three persons.

The lingering question from Sarah and Abraham's encounter, "Is anything too wonderful for the LORD?" is one that can be posed in all Christian education efforts that seek to foster a sense of wonder and awe in response to God. Walter Brueggemann suggests that one possible response in light of biblical faith is, "Everything is not possible, but what God promises is." God's promises are not limited by the readiness of Abraham and Sarah to receive the promise of new life. Brueggemann also suggests that this question "moves to the impossibility of discipleship, the impossibility of faith, and the impossibility of new community," that are also the concerns of Christian education in discerning our encounter with the Triune God.[28] Discipleship, faith, and new community are possible as God's gifts to a fallen and alienated humanity through Jesus Christ as described in the New Testament. It is Jesus, the Second Person of the Trinity, who comes to have table fellowship with all of humanity through his incarnation. God's visitation to Abraham and Sarah finds its fullest expression in the coming of Jesus Christ.

A New Testament Perspective

The Christian claim that God is *for* us is revealed most explicitly in God the Father's giving of Jesus *for* all of us. Over the years John 3:16 is the verse that Sunday school teachers have taught as the gospel in a nutshell: "For God so loved the world that he gave his only Son, so that everyone who believes in him may not perish but may have eternal life." This verse points to the depth of God's love. The awesome extent of God's love and care is the basis for our care for others through our educational ministries. Another New Testament passage that describes the vast extent of God's love and care is Romans 8:31–39:

> What then are we to say about these things? If God is for us, who is against us? He who did not withhold his own Son, but gave him up for all of us, will he not with him also give us everything else? Who will bring any charge against God's elect? It is God who justifies. Who is to condemn? It is Christ Jesus, who died, yes, who was raised, who is at the right hand of God, who indeed intercedes for us. Who will separate us from the love of Christ? Will hardship, or distress, or persecution, or famine, or nakedness, or peril, or sword? As it is written, "For your sake we are being killed all day long; we are accounted as sheep to be slaughtered." No, in all these things we are more than conquerors through him who loved us. For I am convinced that neither death, nor life, nor angels, nor rulers, nor things present, nor things to come, nor powers, nor height, nor depth, nor anything else in all creation, will be able to separate us from the love of God in Christ Jesus our Lord.

Paul's description of the far reach of God's love provides a foundation for understanding the care for others that is extended in teaching. As Karl Barth observed, "If the object of theological knowledge is Jesus Christ and, in him, perfect love, then *Agape* alone can be the dominant and formative prototype and principle of theology."[29] With Christ's love as the norm and pre-eminent theological theme, Christian teachers have a standard to guide their ministries. The life of the Trinity reflects the fullest expression of love as God the Father so loved the world to send the Son who, along with the Father, sends the Spirit. The Spirit, in turn, equips and sends those called as teachers.

Teachers also have a resource promised in verse 32 that implies a challenge to grasp the holistic nature of this love or care for others. Such an understanding can help to avoid a reductionism that seeks a quick fix to every problem or issue before persons, communities, and global society. Care calls for long-term relationships. The search for a quick fix limits the effectiveness of teaching both over time and in the short term.[30] The call for a long-term perspective stands counter to a current preoccupation with quick fixes. An example of the short-term view is the current preoccupation with measurable outcomes at all levels of education. Another example is the preference for single-event workshops that do not allow for transfer of learning, internalization of insight, or various process elements required for transformation in the lives of participants. The emphasis upon love requires a care for the content, persons, and context of Christian education. Trinitarian grammar requires consideration of a larger framework. Likewise, the focus upon love in caring for others, God, and self cannot be divorced from the complementary values of truth, faith, hope, and joy that should shape Christian teaching.[31] The life of the wider community and world are matters of concern because of the nature of created life.

The danger of reductionism as it relates to the Trinity can be considered further. God the Father being for us cannot be divorced from the person and ministry of Jesus Christ and, after his earthly departure, the coming of the Holy Spirit at Pentecost (Acts 1, 2). Romans 5:5 explicitly teaches us that "hope does not disappoint us, because God's love has been poured into our hearts through the Holy Spirit that has been given to us." This fulfills the promise of God the Father to give us everything else in addition to his Son (Rom. 8:32). Karl Barth reminds Christians that the ultimate object of theology is "the living God in the living Jesus Christ and in the Holy Spirit's power of Life."[32]

This spiritual reality of shared life and partnership is best explored in terms of the Trinity.

God for us is best modeled in teaching by considering both the revelation and mystery of the Trinity. LaCugna argues for the need to relate an understanding of the Trinity to the salvific work of God in Jesus' earthly ministry. God being for us is expressed in God's work of salvation for humanity, for the world, for the entire creation. At the very center of God's plan of salvation is relationship as God seeks out humanity. The abundant life intended for humanity is revealed most clearly and gloriously in the life of the Trinity. Understanding and wrestling with the Trinity, just as Jacob wrestled with the angel of the Lord at Peniel (Gen. 32:22–32), is a distinctive of the Christian life that educators must consider in an age of religious pluralism. The Trinity is a reality Christians can offer and share in interreligious discussions of religious education. As Christians, we hold much in common with theists' conceptions about God's importance to the human journey. With Jews and Muslims, we affirm a monotheistic faith. Yet the mystery of the God revealed as three in one and one in three is the distinctive or organizing theme most revolutionary for educational thought and practice. How is this so? Trinitarian grammar and imagination are not new as cited above in the work of Nels Ferré and James Smart. What is new is the rising hunger of generations across many cultures for the relationships and sense of community most clearly modeled in the Trinity. Biblical theology as considered in the Genesis and Romans passages leads us to consider the centrality of the Trinity as a theological grounding for the thought and practice of Christian education in the third millennia.

Trinitarian Educational Imagination

The use of trinitarian grammar and imagination in relation to educational foundations affirms the multiple-level understanding possible in this doctrine for all of life. Archbishop William Temple suggested that to worship is "to purge the imagination by the beauty of God."[33] The beauty of the Christian God is revealed most wondrously in the Trinity. The Trinity affirms a diversity of three along with a unity that brings wholeness and integration. Max L. Stackhouse suggests that a full appreciation of the theological Trinity implies a tripartite analysis of various areas of human experience, including education. A tripartite or trinitarian imagination and analysis propose neither uniformity nor unending plurality, but rather unity amid a limited diversity that is best modeled for humanity in the community of Creator, Redeemer, and Sustainer of the one true God.[34] Persons are created in the image of the Triune God, and the fullness of humanity is best understood in considering God's Son incarnated in the person of Jesus Christ.

In my own earlier work, I have proposed an educational trinity that defines education as the process of sharing *content* with *persons* in the *context* of their community and society. The educational trinity of content, persons, and context serves as an underlying form of Christian education.[35] Historically, educational battles have been waged as to which of these three elements should have priority in educational practice. Trinitarian imagination that embraces all three has avoided the inevitable reductionism that stresses one or even two of these essentials to the exclusion of others.[36] Beyond the consideration of an educational trinity of content, persons, and context, what more can be proposed for teaching practice? In responding to an initial draft of this work, Eileen Starr insightfully suggested the three emphases of unity in diversity, relationships of love, and purposeful joint action as flowing from my work. These categories parallel those that are noted in the Chalcedonian form or grammar used to describe the person of Jesus Christ and discussed in chapter 3.

The insights of Stackhouse affirm the importance of the Trinity for the place of unity in a limited diversity. The essentials of unity and diversity themselves are subject to debate and conflict in educational practice. Educators who stress unity within the fallen human condition are subject to succumb to a press for uniformity and conformity that fail to honor the diversity present in creation. Chalcedonian form affirms differentiation. In considering the disclosure of God most fully in Jesus Christ, Scripture itself provides us with four portraits of Jesus in the Gospels. Educators who stress diversity within the fallen human condition are subject to succumb to a press for endless plurality and fragmentation that fail to honor the unity present in creation. The disclosure of one God affirmed in Christian faith attests to the unity of all humanity as God's creatures and accountability in relation to the whole of creation. Chalcedonian form affirms unity.

Relationships of love as revealed in the Trinity require our fulfillment of the two great commandments—to love God with all of our hearts, souls, minds, and strength and to love our neighbors as ourselves. I propose that these commandments provide the foundation for the basics of teaching as presented in my earlier work.[37] Chalcedonian form affirms order, and Jesus' commandments demonstrate an order of loves that gives priority to God and then others without loss of self. Rather, loving God and others fosters the finding of one's true self. Teaching also wrestles with the inevitable conflicts that persons confront in fulfilling these commandments in their lives. The issues of public versus private or personal commitments present challenges for living the Christian faith in the world. The expression of social love demands of Christians a commitment to justice and righteousness along with peace for all of God's creatures, most particularly those who have been marginalized and neglected. The real limits of resources and time require that difficult choices be made and priorities be set. Love implies educational choices regarding content shared so that persons are engaged within their particular historical, social, cultural, economic, political, religious, and ideological contexts. Patterns of power and authority ought to be considered in teaching if love embraces the wider social situation.[38]

Purposeful conjoint action affirms the place of collaborative and cooperative action in teaching practice. The reality of the Trinity implies a commitment to community beyond the self-interest that plagues humanity in general and American culture in particular. Perichoresis implies a joint and interdependent life that requires a transformation of the human heart to embrace the human community. A prophetic stance is required in Christian teaching to enable persons to embrace the tasks of advocacy and service as central to the gospel message of new life in Christ. Christ restores in humanity the image of the Triune God that was distorted by sin. This restoration makes possible collaborative and cooperative action through persons via the transformative ministry of the Holy Spirit who encounters human spirits. For postmodern settings, the Christian church's practices in public life reveal the authenticity of faith claims as persons search for genuine community revealed in the life of the Trinity. Beyond these three emphases, what more might be suggested for teaching practice emerging from a consideration of the Trinity?

An Exploration of Educational Implications

Trinitarian grammar and imagination can be further explored by considering how theorists and practitioners in the field have drawn upon it in addressing certain perennial educational questions. A survey of tripartite analyses serves to place my proposals in the broader educational discussion and to provide supportive evidence for the generative possibilities of trinitarian grammar and imagination for teaching. Discerning the value of tripartite analyses involves their correlation with biblical and theological foundations and their generativity in relation to perennial educational questions and teaching practice. Perennial educational questions consider the what, why, how, where, when, and who of Christian education.[39] An additional question most recently suggested by D. Campbell Wyckoff is, in what atmosphere does Christian education take place? Wyckoff's response is in an atmosphere of prayer coupled with justice and love. This additional question deals with the ethos—the tone, quality, or character of common life—or the affective area of human experience.[40] Atmosphere or ethos can be explored in relation to the type of life modeled by the Trinity that includes love, justice, prayer, and a host of other Christian virtues that can guide human interaction.

The *what* question regarding the nature of education is addressed in my proposed definition of education as a process of sharing content with persons in the context of their community and society. The three educational elements of *content, persons,* and *context* provide one way of understanding the nature of education. God as the creator is the educator from whom all the *content* of education issues. Jesus as the exemplar or mentor is the model, the Master Teacher, who in his *person* exemplifies all that a teacher should be. The Holy Spirit as the tutor is the counselor or community consultant who sustains the life of the Christian community and the wider society (*context*) in ways that fulfill God's purposes.[41] In *The Liberating Spirit,* Eldin Villafañe explores how the Spirit anoints the Christian community for its social ministry, enabling the church to confront the principalities and powers of society with a message of hope and transformation related to the biblical agenda of *shalom.*[42]

The *why* question of purposes or goals has been addressed by a number of educational theorists. In particular, I find the insights of Susanne Johnson, Marianne Sawicki, and Lois LeBar to be generative for guiding educational practice as reported by students engaged in various teaching ministries. It may be significant that these women provide greater sensitivity to educational practices through the experience of connection and the value of relationships that generally characterize female development. Johnson proposes the three dynamic processes of worship, praxis, and instruction for Christian formation.[43] Sawicki analyzes historical developments in Christian education in terms of the gospel's expression of call, cult (or celebration), and care. In other words, direct proclamation of the Word, prayerful celebration of sacrament, and caring service to human need provide a trinitarian grammar for understanding teaching.[44] Johnson's worship, praxis, and instruction parallel Sawicki's celebration (cult), care, and call. LeBar's three goals present these same purposes in more evangelistic and missional terms related to the person of Jesus Christ. LeBar proposes to bring persons to Christ (proclamation); to build them up in Christ (edification); and to send them out into the world for Christ (mission).[45]

The *how* question of methods can be considered in relation to what Julie Gorman has referred to as the "triple crown of teaching."[46] The triple crown in this case is what I identify as the preparation, instruction, and evaluation of teaching.[47] Certainly, other tripartite forms have been proposed such as the trilogy of

James Michael Lee involving the shape, flow, and content of religious instruction.[48] Identification of one particular formula or proposal is not stressed, but rather the values that a tripartite analysis can provide for educational thought and practice. Peter Hodgson, in developing his theology of education that focuses on *paideia* as God's wisdom offered to humanity, identifies three basic elements: critical thinking, heightened imagination, and liberating practice. These three relate to my educational trinity in that critical thinking relates to *content*, heightened imagination to *persons'* creativity, and liberating practice to the *context* of the community and society. The three elements form a rhythm and cycle of teaching. Hodgson also points out that other scholars have arranged a similar tripartite designation of pedagogical elements.[49]

The questions of context *(where)* and readiness *(when)* generally have not lent themselves to tripartite emphases except for the formulas of home, church, and school in the case of educational contexts and past, present, and future in relation to readiness. These areas suggest that a threefold category can be proposed and may be helpful, but is not required in either educational thought or practice.

The final question of *who* has often been divided according to children, youth, and adults when analyzing the persons engaged in Christian education. Beyond these obvious categories, Margaret Ann Crain identifies three qualities of Christian education that is effective and mutual: "(1) the educator must see herself or himself as an interpreter among interpreters; (2) the contexts for learning must create hospitable and just space; and (3) the congregation must practice the presence of God."[50] Crain's insights are suggestive for the type of persons who should be teaching. A Christian teacher should be open, welcoming, and spiritual and be in a community that honors these values with all persons. Again, these qualities or ideals reflect the life of the Trinity that Christian educators hope to replicate in their relationships with others. Beyond these qualities, Karl Barth points out one additional qualification for the Christian educator: "Only by his qualification as a learner can he show himself qualified to become a teacher."[51]

Beyond the particulars of these perennial educational questions, the Trinity provides me with the key organizing theme for exploring the personal and communal nature of relationships fostered in Christian education.[52] This organizing theme has universal implications from the perspective of Christian claims. In relation to Christian personal life, the three essential anchors for identity are that each person is potentially a child of God, a sister or brother of Jesus Christ, and a vessel for the Holy Spirit. These provide a basis for developing a theological anthropology.[53] Growth in understanding and living out these relationships provides the substance for Christian education that stresses discipleship and spiritual formation. In relation to Christian communal life, the three essential anchors for identity are that persons corporately are the people of God, the body of Christ, and the temple of the Holy Spirit. The processes of Christian formation, edification, and mission emerge from the relationships that the Christian faith community has with the Trinity. The task of any teaching ministry is to balance these emphases upon the corporate and personal dimensions of life in complementary ways.

Conclusion

This chapter has explored the generative connection between the theological basis of the Trinity and the ministries of teaching. Other theological realities call for our attention, including the gap that exists between the Trinity and our human condition. This gap is also called sin and is the subject of chapter 2.

The essential teaching emphasized in the first chapter is the following: the Triune God being *for* us is the essential starting point for understanding the theological foundation of Christian education. This starting point recognizes the continual place of mystery, wonder, and awe in relationship to God and of partnership with God in teaching. Mystery, wonder, and awe are associated with our response to the Trinity. Nevertheless, the Triune God initiates a relationship that is for us. In being for us, the implication for teaching is the central place of love and care.

Because God cares for us, we care for others in our teaching ministries. God teaches us most particularly through revelation as Trinity. Christian education strives to bring persons "face to face with God"[54] revealed as Trinity in the person of Jesus Christ through the ministry of the Holy Spirit.

TWO

GOD DESPITE US:
SIN AND SALVATION

With the affirmation of God being *for* us in the Christian teaching of the Trinity, we may be led to complacency bathing in the light of God's grace. The human situation poses problems in the reception of grace, mercy, and love as revealed in the persons and life of the Triune God. The Christian faith describes the primary problem as sin that causes a great divorce or separation between the creator God and humanity. The effects of sin extend to a world that groans in anticipating the full salvation God intends for humanity and all of creation (Rom. 8:18–30).

Despite this great gulf between humanity and God, God has decisively acted in the coming of Jesus Christ to offer salvation and new life where death in its various expressions would otherwise reign supreme. The coming of God's kingdom in Christ offers hope for a hopeless dilemma that God alone can remedy. God's provision in the face of human and ecological despair represents the good news of the gospel. This gospel is worthy of universal proclamation in the preaching and teaching ministries of the Christian church. The mission of Christian education is vitally linked with the church's effort to declare in word and deed the wonders of the gospel to a world destined for despair and destruction because of sin. Despite the realities and far-reaching effects of sin, the Triune God works to fulfill the purposes of creation in a new creation made available through Jesus Christ. The penultimate and ultimate ends of God's providential care stand in contrast to the contours of sin that impact the human situation. However, before rushing to the reconciliation God offers, Christians must first consider the nature and extent of sin.

An Introduction to Sin

Sin is not a popular topic for polite and educated society. However, sin results in a loss of relationship with the Trinity, the source of life, and a loss of trinitarian imagination. Sin is a failure to fulfill God's purposes and will for life. Psychiatrist Karl Menninger wrote the work *Whatever Became of Sin?* in considering the often avoided topic of sin.[1] Despite our reluctance to address sin, Christians find biblical and theological warrant to understand its depths in order to better appreciate the extent of God's grace as suggested in Romans 5:20: "But where sin increased, grace abounded all the more."

An appreciation of the person and current work of the Holy Spirit also leads us to grapple with sin. In John 16:7–11 Jesus describes the work of the Spirit as being in continuity with his earthly ministry:

> Nevertheless I tell you the truth: it is to your advantage that I go away, for if I do not go away, the Advocate will not come to you; but if I go, I will send him to you. And when he comes, he will prove the world wrong about sin and righteousness and judgment: about sin, because they do not believe in me; about righteousness, because I am going to the Father and you will see me no longer; about judgment, because the ruler of this world has been condemned.

The curriculum set for the Advocate or Holy Spirit in Jesus' projection includes sin, righteousness, and judgment. Sin serves to describe the human dilemma that is experienced both personally and corporately. The corporate reality of sin means that consideration must be given to how persons have been sinned against. It also means that persons are responsible for their complicity with corporate patterns of oppression and injustice that remain unaddressed. Corporate patterns of sin result in privilege and power accruing to certain persons at the expense of others, perpetuating socially acceptable forms of prejudice, deference, and victimization. At times, addressing these corporate patterns occurs without regard to one's personal sin and responsibility. In similar fashion, a personal preoccupation might exclude consideration of corporate sin. This suggests that sin is pervasive enough to affect every area of our personal and corporate lives, requiring explicit teaching and disciplined introspection and confession. The Scriptures suggest as much in 1 John 1:9–10: "If we confess our sins, he who is faithful and just will forgive us our sins and cleanse us from all unrighteousness. If we say that we have not sinned, we make him a liar, and his word is not in us." Therefore, the initial response to the matter of sin requires a stark honesty about ourselves and the patterns of our social interaction. The extent of sin often remains at unconscious levels and requires the work of the Holy Spirit to disclose the gaps between God and us. Only with conscious recognition of sin comes the possibility of forgiveness and cleansing.

The matter of sin calls us into a position of radical accountability before a holy and just God. This flows from an appreciation of the creation and our positions of dependency upon God. God as creator makes demands upon humanity and has clear expectations for how we ought to live. These demands are in keeping with God's provisions for the human condition and all of creation. This is a source of wonder and awe in considering the extent of grace and mercy that finds expression in the gift of God's very own Son. The greatest fulfillment for humanity and the creation comes in breaching the gulf caused by sin through God's ministries of restoration. The wonder of this gift deepens with the realization that God's love is extended even while we stand in stark rebellion against the creator and lover of our very souls. The incarnation demonstrates the extent of God's love in that without the assurance of human response, God was willing to risk his Son in redeeming a lost humanity.

Following this introduction, I explore the nature of sin by returning to the trinitarian imagination analyzed in chapter 1.

Sin analyzed in relation to God the Father, Son, and Spirit provides insights for Christian education. A discussion of sin indicates that Christian educators must attend to matters of amoral development in both theory and practice. I discuss aspects of amoral development in my work *Foundational Issues in Christian Education* when I consider the psychological foundations of Christian education.[2]

Sin and God the Father

The matter of sin in relation to God the Father points out the contrast between God's holiness and human depravity. The Reformed doctrine of total depravity does not suggest that persons are totally without any redeemable quality or that they are the worst possible in all dimensions of their lives and beings. It does suggest that all aspects of human life are affected by sin. It also suggests that though the very image of God is distorted in persons, that image is not obliterated. Restoration of the image is possible through God's gracious intervention in history through Jesus Christ. The remaining vestige of God's image also suggests that persons are still accountable to God for their responses to the offer of salvation, which itself is a gift. Persons who depend upon God's turning of their fallen wills, hearts, and minds for salvation stand accountable before a merciful and gracious creator who seeks the restoration and advance of creation. Though sin's impacts are pervasive, the possibility of transformation looms.

Teaching the holiness of God as contrasted with sin brings about concern for a renewal of worth and dignity. Perry Downs proposes three implications for Christian education that flow from a consideration of God's holiness and humanity's sin. First, we understand that "unredeemed people cannot understand spiritual truth"; second, "there must be supernatural intervention in our ministry for lives to be touched"; and third, "Christian education is a partnership between God and the educator."[3] These implications require educators to exercise dependence upon God through prayer and spiritual discernment if teaching is to restore the worth and dignity of persons through spiritual transformation. When persons encounter the awesome and holy God of Christianity, their human alienation is transformed into new life and possibility. God chooses to use the foolishness of Christian teaching and preaching to offer salvation to alienated humanity as a remedy for sin and its devastating consequences.

Sin and God the Son

The coming of Jesus the Christ marks God's historical intervention to remedy the problem of sin. He who knew no sin became as sin to redeem fallen humanity and restore right relationships between God and persons. Second Corinthians 5:20–21 makes this explicit: "So we are ambassadors for Christ, since God is making his appeal through us; we entreat you on behalf of Christ, be reconciled to God. For our sake he made him to be sin who knew no sin, so that in him we might become the righteousness of God." Christ's righteousness is made available to persons because of his willingness to be sin and to suffer its eternal consequences. Christian educators participate in this ministry of reconciliation through teaching that centers on the person and work of Jesus Christ. Ronald Habermas and Klaus Issler propose that reconciliation be the central theme for Christian education. The reconciliation themes they propose are communion, community, character, and commission. Communion involves "praising God by acknowledging and obeying" God's "revelation." Community involves "experiencing genuine fellowship through the common bond of Christ." Character involves "being individually nurtured to grow into the Son's image." The full restoration of God's image in persons is possible through their relationship with Jesus Christ. Commission involves "sharing the good news of Christ's love; ministering to needy people; applying God's truth to life and vocation."[4]

The renewal of the worth and dignity of persons in countering the effects of sin takes curricular form in Habermas and Issler's themes for reconciliation. These themes extend the ministry of Jesus Christ into contemporary contexts, as they address the needs of various age groups in addition to the total life of Christian congregations. The problem of sin is addressed in the ministry of Jesus Christ and extended to his followers through their educational ministries of reconciliation.

Sin and God the Spirit

The ministry of the Holy Spirit as described in John 16:7–11 centers on the curricular themes of sin, righteousness, and judgment. Sin is a necessary theme because the world did not believe in Jesus. The lack of belief in Jesus relates to the first implication that Downs identified: "Unredeemed people cannot understand spiritual truth."[5] The work of the Holy Spirit is essential in the hearts, minds, spirits, and wills of persons if they are to be drawn to and believe in Jesus the Christ. God's holiness and righteousness revealed most fully in Jesus stand in stark contrast with human sin. Human culpability and depravity confront persons in relation to their personal and corporate sin. Such recognition exposes persons to their immediate and ultimate vulnerability before a righteous and holy God. Spiritual eyes need to be opened for such a disclosure. The Holy Spirit speaks to the spirits of persons across their life spans in offering new life that flows from the Trinity.[6] The disclosure of sin directly relates to the righteousness of God revealed in Christ and to God's judgment upon sin. Sin maintains a stance of autonomy, a refusal to recognize Gods' authority. Such a stance results in spiritual death and ultimate alienation from God's purposes for humanity and all of creation. In relation to Christian education, the work of teachers in partnership with the Holy Spirit is to confront the reality of sin and to pose the problems it presents. This requires caring enough to confront the nature and extent of sin.

The other themes of the Spirit's ministry as described by Jesus include righteousness and judgment. In relation to righteousness, teachers are encouraged to educate for responsible action. This challenge is most explicit in the work of Nicholas Wolterstorff. Wolterstorff proposes the best way for Christian values to be internalized and supported through education. A person (parent, teacher, friend) is to act lovingly toward a child and to "combine discipline and modeling with the enunciation of a moral standard which the child perceives to fit the situations and on which he or she is willing to act."[7] The internalization of values contributes to works of righteousness and can lead to responsible action in Christian education. The place of judgment requires discernment to distinguish the sense intended. Judgment understood as evaluation is affirmed (1 Cor. 2:15) by those who are spiritual, but judgment understood as condemnation is prohibited (Matt. 7:1–4; Luke 6:37). The positive aspect of judgment relates to discernment, which itself is a spiritual gift, but the condemnation of others involves a lack of love and is offensive to God. Education implies the fostering of discernment, and spiritual education implies the fostering of spiritual discernment. The work of the Holy Spirit is essential for encouraging spiritual discernment since the Spirit discloses the gaps between God's offer of life and aspects of human existence. In relation to sin, spiritual discernment can point to the Christian hope of a remedy. Sinful patterns need not remain as they are, for God's resources are made available in Jesus Christ. Alternatives are possible because God's grace operates at the limits of human possibility. This is worth celebrating and sharing. Christian teaching can witness to God's transformative power made available through the Holy Spirit. God works *despite* us, despite human sin in corporate and individual life to bring reconciliation, healing, and wholeness.

Sin and Teaching

How does sin impact the ministries of teaching? One obvious way is that when persons are involved, sin is a given. Any perfect teaching setting changes when I am present because I am a sinner. Being a sinner and interacting with others sinners, I am aware of the potential for sinful patterns to emerge that can result in the oppression of others. The extent of oppression can vary greatly according to the levels of dysfunctionality present. The challenge for the teacher and all participants is to reduce the potential for dysfunction and to encourage a liberating or transformative educational experience for all. Nevertheless, the potential for misunderstanding, offending, or squelching persons remains.

A dependence upon the operation of God's grace is essential at every stage of the teaching process. Those stages include preparation, instruction, and evaluation.[8] Sin emerges in failing to accomplish God's purposes or will in any of these stages. Diligence is required of both teachers and students if the impact of sin is to be minimized and the salvific blessings of Christ's ministry applied. One Old Testament model for such diligence is Ezra, who serves as the scholar/priest active in the life of the community. The complementary teaching ministries of the Levites support his teaching ministry as described in Nehemiah 8. Their combined ministries result in renewal of the entire community returning from exile. The lay ministry of Nehemiah himself supported the community in its return to Jerusalem.[9] Ezra's ministry served as an example of diligence, dedication, and devotion as described in Ezra 7:10. Ezra dedicated himself to the three tasks of studying, living, and teaching God's Word in the life of the faith community. Ezra's example is noteworthy and appropriate for those who serve under the new covenant of Jesus' ministry and the priesthood he initiated (1 Peter 2:1–10).

The matter of sin directly relates to the inevitable tension between freedom and form in teaching. Because of sin and its potential, form is required to provide discipline and control in an educational setting. Real limits exist, and to benefit from the teaching opportunity, a certain level of control is required that assures the well-being and protection of all participants. If extreme, such control can restrict freedom and squelch learning. If appropriate, the control of internalized discipline enhances expression and creativity in teaching. The maturity and readiness of participants influence the level of discipline required or even the need for explicit intervention to assert the authority of teachers as gatekeepers for the teaching-learning process. The level of creativity fostered in the teaching itself affects the need for external limits or constraints. The other dynamic operative in teaching is the participation of students in setting ground rules or limits, which again is subject to their level of maturity. Beyond the question of maturity, any teaching situation is served by clarifying the underlying form in order to restrain or constrain sin.

The complement to any discussion of form is the issue of freedom or liberation. Freedom in teaching and learning should not lead to license, but to full participation in the invitation implied in teaching. The invitation is to discovery, dialogue, and even drama. Discovery is the potential for participants to consider their interests, questions, and needs. Dialogue makes possible the sharing of questions, issues, and insights in the communal search for truth and wisdom. Drama is possible as persons assume their roles in both the immediate setting and in the larger narratives of life. These larger narratives include the family, community, and wider society. The ultimate narrative embraces God's story, which for Christians includes the redemption story.[10] Drama makes possible the honoring of various gifts bestowed upon the participants and the trying on of new roles. It also allows space for the presence and ministry of the Holy Spirit to direct the teaching encounters in new and unexpected ways.

In their discussion of sin, Gabriel and Dorothy Fackre identify the issues of idolatry, arrogance, and apathy.[11] Idolatry relates to the matters of purposes and goals in both education and life. To what ends are human energies devoted? What educational outcomes guide participants? From a Christian perspective, the ultimate purposes are the glory and enjoyment of God. Penultimate purposes include the discovery of truth and the encouragement of love or care. By contrast, various idolatries focus upon the created instead of the creator and other purposes that can be in conflict with God's will. In relation to idolatry, Christian teachers consider confrontation and the proposal of alternatives.

Arrogance involves "lording it over" others and self-righteousness at the expense of others.[12] This abuse of power stands in contrast to the cooperative and supportive relationships modeled for humanity in the Trinity as discussed in chapter 1. Christian teaching calls for a teachable spirit and the valuing of others in addition to oneself. The Apostle Paul describes that spirit in Philippians 2:3–4: "Do nothing from selfish ambition or conceit, but in humility regard others as better than yourselves. Let each of you look not to your own interests, but to the interests of others."

Apathy and various forms of escape into sensuality are patterns of the human landscape.[13] Apathy is a lack of care and contrasts with the care God intends for the content, persons, and context of teaching. The misuse of freedom and the possible misdirection of motivation can be educational issues. Christian teaching can serve to form persons for responsible freedom and direction in their lives. First John 2:15–17 describes the choices:

> Do not love the world or the things in the world. The love of the Father is not in those who love the world; for all that is in the world—the desire of the flesh, the desire of the eyes, the pride in riches—comes not from the Father but from the world. And the world and its desire are passing away, but those who do the will of God live forever.

The "world" in this case refers to the world system that stands in rebellion against God and contrary to God's will and purposes. The choice posed is between love of the creator and love of the created. Prophetic Christian teaching may pose choices for persons in terms of the life offered by God and the ultimate death related to "the desire of the flesh, the desire of the eyes, the pride in riches" (or the pride of life). World, flesh, desire, and pride are associated with sin and its consequences in the human situation. Christian teaching identifies alternatives and encourages responsible choices.

Related to sin and teaching are the matters of temptation, guilt, conscience, repentance, and forgiveness in Christian theology. Temptation is a reality with the potential for sin in human life. Teaching provides an opportunity to help persons avoid temptation in response to the prayer "lead us not into temptation." Moral education can provide an incentive to assist persons in their responses to temptation by exploring alternative responses that fulfill God's purposes and will. Guilt is recognizing one's responsibility before God and others in relation to sin and its expression. Christian teaching can assist persons to distinguish real guilt from false guilt. The place of conscience and its development is a matter in the formative dimension of education. Raising the consciousness of sin relates to both the personal and corporate areas of life. A corporate consciousness of sin calls for the recognition of those who have been sinned against. In the recognition of sin comes the call for repentance in Christian teaching and the offer of forgiveness made possible through the provision of Jesus Christ. Related to repentance are the issues of restitution and restorative justice in social life.

Salvation: God For Us, Despite Us

Despite the reality of sin and its pervasive affects, God's stance for us prevails. It prevails in the offer of salvation that the Trinity avails to all of creation and humanity. The connection between salvation and education is explored through a scheme proposed by Lawrence Richards to guide creative Bible teaching (with one addition). Richards proposed a *hook, book, look,* and *took* scheme to guide lesson planning. Many educators have used this method over the years, most recently La Verne Tolbert.[14] The *hook* is an approach to a teaching lesson that draws in and interests the participants. The *book* is the presentation of a biblical story, theme, or concept. The *look* is the exploration of the material's implications and applications for the lives of the participants. The *took* is the suggestion of and commitment to actual responses on the part of participants in the light of what has been learned or discovered. The addition I make to the order is *cook: hook, book, look, cook,* and *took.*[15] These five teaching movements are parallel with the five theological categories associated with salvation: prevenient grace, justification, sanctification, edification, and glorification. The resulting paired connections are: prevenient grace—hook, justification—book, sanctification—look, edification—cook, and glorification—took. These pairings provide one means by which to connect salvation to teaching. Other forms of analysis are possible, including James Loder's proposal for a logic of the Spirit,[16] but these five connections directly link theological insights to actual teaching.

Prevenient Grace—Hook

Prevenient grace refers to the gracious drawing of persons to saving faith before their conscious embrace of Jesus Christ. The Holy Spirit works subtly and mysteriously in the hearts, minds, and affections of persons to bring awareness of sin, righteousness, and judgment (John 16:7–11). The Holy Spirit provides a foretaste of the salvation offered in Jesus Christ through contact with Christian persons who evidence a new life. The Spirit also uses the preaching and teaching of Scripture to awaken a spiritual hunger that will only be satisfied by encountering the living Christ. As the great North African teacher Augustine suggested, our hearts are restless until they find their rest in God.[17] The prayers of believers help to foster an openness that can hook persons in imperceptible ways. God's Spirit works to enliven the spirits of those who remain insensitive to spiritual matters.

The operation of prevenient grace relates to Downs's first two implications that flow from God's holiness: "unredeemed people cannot understand spiritual truth," and "there must be supernatural intervention in our ministry for lives to be touched."[18] Prevenient grace refers to the requisite supernatural intervention for the understanding of spiritual truth. God graciously draws persons to consider their need and find rest for their restless souls. Prevenient grace brings persons to a point where they can pray that ancient prayer, "Lord Jesus Christ, Son of the Living God, have mercy on me a sinner." Jesus is one who can take away the sins of the world and offer pardon and peace. Receptivity to Jesus follows from a stance of repentance in relation to sin. Beyond the pardon, persons are eventually brought to a point of praising a holy God with eternal hosannas. This alone is fitting for those created by God to give honor, glory, and praise to their creator. Prevenient grace opens a place of wonder and awe that touches the deepest longings of the human heart and mind while recognizing the place of mystery. Prevenient grace is the hook that draws persons to God just as a lesson's hook invites learners to discover new truth and life that issues from it.

The work of prevenient grace requires teachers to pray for participants in any educational opportunity. Prayer focuses on intercession for students and petition for teachers themselves. Intercession longs for the partnering work of the Holy Spirit in the lives of participants that they may be open to the truths and experiences that God calls them to embrace. Petition expresses the teachers' reliance upon God to work through preparation, instruction, and subsequent evaluation.[19] This ministry of prayer makes a difference and can be shared with other Christians in any setting. For example, the regular and faithful intercession of prayer warriors in the Second Spanish Baptist Church in East Harlem, New York, sustained an effective youth ministry that resulted in transformed lives. I never want to forget this lesson in the operation of prevenient grace, for it demonstrates the power of God to work in teaching and other forms of ministry.

Justification—Book

Sin requires a judgment "by the book" and a settling of accounts. Christ's offer of salvation becomes real as persons individually and corporately receive it. Christ's justification has universal implications for the restoration of creation. The recognition of Christ's offer is confirmed through the teaching and preaching of the most wonderful of all books, the Bible. The witness of the Scriptures is to the saving power of Jesus Christ in radically addressing the problem of sin. Pardon and forgiveness make possible a new relationship with a holy and all-consuming God. Our sins are removed as far as the east is from the west (Ps. 103:12) because of God's steadfast love. The extent of God's love finds expression in the incarnation, life, death, and resurrection of Jesus Christ. Jesus' provision for sin contrasts with all personal and corporate human efforts of self-righteousness. The stark judgment of the Scriptures is that all such human efforts equal an effort to cover or justify ourselves with filthy rags or cloth (Isa. 64:6). God's remedy for sin and guilt is found in the justification by faith offered in Jesus Christ: "Therefore, since we are justified by faith, we have peace with God through our Lord Jesus Christ, through whom we have obtained access to this grace in which we stand; and we boast in our hope of sharing the glory of God" (Rom. 5:1–2). This core Christian teaching represents the good news of the gospel that brings liberation. What humankind could not accomplish in relationship to God is possible in Jesus the Christ.

God's gift of salvation is further explained by the Apostle Paul: "For by grace you have been saved through faith, and this is not your own doing; it is the gift of God—not the result of works, so that no one may boast. For we are what he has made us, created in Christ Jesus for good works, which God prepared beforehand to be our way of life" (Eph. 2:8–10). Justification as God's indescribable and wondrous gift (2 Cor. 9:15), though unrelated to human efforts, is related to a way of life involving good works. Such good works relate to the additional phases of salvation, namely sanctification and edification. Christian teaching points to the justification gifted to humanity in Jesus Christ, but directly encourages the processes of sanctification and edification in the lives of believers. All such connections of teaching with salvation are dependent on the partnership between the Holy Spirit as the divine tutor and human teachers. In relation to justification, Christian teachers can foster a sense of wonder and awe regarding God's gift of Jesus Christ and Jesus' own willingness to endure the cross to offer salvation.

The connection with the *book* relates most directly to the disclosure of the Scriptures and God's special revelation in Jesus Christ. However, it can be extended in a secondary sense to include God's general revelation in creation and human experience. All of creation groans and the breach of sin in the fall affects "nature and supernature, as well as human nature."[20] The extent of justification will eventually affect nature and supernature in the consummation, but glimpses may be revealed in the renewal of nature and the spiritual transformations in supernature. These serve as foretastes of a realized eschatology that can be revelatory for Christian teaching. One striking example of this comes from my recent visit to mainland China. The ravages of the Cultural Revolution could not squelch the vitality of the Christian church and its current efforts to bring renewal to the land and people. The prayers of the Chinese Christians and their sisters and brothers globally mark a spiritual turning point in the advance of the gospel. This is a sign of the justification in Christ that issues in new life as many persons come to faith. With a renewed faith, persons are active in the renewal of the land and wider society. Alternatives to amoral development are made possible through the transformative ministry of the Spirit of Christ within faith communities. The spiritual vigor of the church in both its evangelistic and social outreach is a clear witness to the power of Jesus Christ. The experience of being justified by faith leads to a grappling with the dynamics of sanctification.[21]

Sanctification—Look

Salvation involves seeing the light of the gospel, and the verb *look* suggests looking for the full implications of the gospel's light in the world. Here the world is not viewed as that system in opposition to God, but rather all of creation as the object of God's love in the sending of Jesus (John 3:16). Gabriel Fackre points out that "salvation in Scripture, according to the venerable Cruden's *Concordance*, is from 'trouble or danger' as well as 'from sin and its consequences.'" The troubles and dangers in today's context include "oppression, war, poverty, hunger, crime, sickness, sorrow, loneliness, ignorance . . . all the social, economic, political, and personal maladies of our time."[22] Therefore, much in the world calls for the careful gaze or look of Christians. Beyond the looking, the call is for care, service, advocacy, and mission. With a focus on sanctification, individual Christians consider their particular callings or vocations while looking for the implications of salvation in personal life. James Fowler helpfully elaborates upon the consequences of understanding our lives in terms of a Christian calling or vocation:

- We realize that our vocational callings are unique. Competition with others is reduced.
- We are freed from the anxiety that someone else might fulfill our particular callings.
- We rejoice in God's grace and favor in others, and we are not threatened by them.
- We are freed from the false guilt to be "all things to all people." We find comfort in God's plan that we each have a task to perform.

- We are released from self-vindicating thoughts and behavior. We do not need to prove our worth. We seek the balance of time and energy in all of life's responsibilities (family, culture, and church).
- The tyranny of time itself no longer incarcerates us. We are given God's grace in life—even in death.[23]

The clarifying of one's calling comes through the process of sanctification. As contrasted with edification that focuses on corporate life, sanctification considers the individual Christian and his or her walk of faith. Whereas justification traditionally centers on the gift of Christ's past salvific blessings for Christians, sanctification centers on the gift of Christ's present salvific blessings. Glorification in turn centers on the gift of Christ's future salvific blessings. In temporal terms, Christians have been saved (justification), are being saved (sanctification and edification), and will be saved (glorification). For teaching itself, this perspective calls for a consideration of past, present, and future aspects of both corporate and personal experiences of salvation in a holistic fashion.

The *look* of sanctification encourages Christians to consider the operation of God's grace in their spiritual lives. Christians need to be discerning how they practice various spiritual disciplines. One's particular spiritual giftedness or disposition influences the choice of spiritual disciplines. John Westerhoff draws upon the work of Urban Holmes in proposing a typology of spirituality mapped in four quadrants. Four spiritual types are identified: (1) speculative-kataphatic, (2) affective-kataphatic, (3) affective-apophatic, and (4) speculative-apophatic. The speculative pole primarily stresses the mind, and its complement, the affective, primarily stresses the heart. These are the two complementary ends of spiritual life and should not be viewed as dualistic. The synthesis of mind and heart is stressed in a Christian perspective. The apophatic pole stresses direct knowing, and its complement, the kataphatic, stresses indirect knowing. These are the two complementary means of spiritual life.

The speculative-kataphatic type of spirituality can be identified as sacramental. "Its primary aim is to aid persons in fulfilling their vocation in the world. Its major concerns are the discernment of God's will, the discernment of spirits, the imitation of Jesus, and becoming aware of God's presence and action in human life and history."[24] The affective-kataphatic can be identified as charismatic. "Its primary aim is to achieve holiness of life. Its major concerns are friendship with Jesus, an outpouring of the Holy Spirit, and providing a sign of God's reign through personal and communal life."[25] The affective-apophatic can be identified as mystical. "Its primary aim is to be united with God. . . . Its major concerns are pointing to the reality of God's reign and abiding in that reality."[26] The speculative-apophatic can be identified as apostolic. "Its primary aim is to obey God's will completely. . . . Its major concerns are witness to God's reign and striving for justice and peace."[27] Each of the four spiritual types complements the others and is important for the holistic ministry of the Christian church.

Knowing one's spiritual type does not exclude gaining from a stretch of spiritual practice in other spiritual quadrants or forms. For Christian teaching this implies the need for a variety of spiritual practices to address the variety of persons in any one setting. Westerhoff defines spiritual life as a love affair with God.[28] The two great commandments propose how this love finds expression for Christians. Love of God engages all of the heart, mind, soul, and strength, which is the focus of sanctification. This is the first great commandment. The second is to love our neighbor as ourselves—that is the focus of edification.

Edification—Cook

Shelly Cunningham proposes the addition of *cook* to Richards's scheme of *hook, book, look,* and *took.* Apart from my emphasis here, Cunningham sees *cook* as the final step of learning that fosters the follow-up or transfer of learning after one teaching session and prior to its successive session.[29] My use of *cook* links up with the opportunity to interact intentionally with dialogue among participants. To cook allows participants to place their ingredients in a common pot that enables the active sharing of flavors and textures. The product of such interaction is a dish distinct from all the separate individual ingredients.

The use of a cooking metaphor suggests the essential interactive and corporate dimension of the Christian community that is too readily forgotten in the United States with its emphasis on individualism and personalism devoid of communal commitments. The Christian church is a corporate reality, and the place of edification, of being built up together in Christ, must be renewed in Christian teaching. For teaching itself, this suggests a need for cooperative and collaborative work and an awareness beyond individual interests and needs. Abraham Heschel, the Jewish educator, warned of the tyranny of needs that plagued the United States.[30] A religious alternative involves the disclosure of God's demands that serves to place in perspective any individual needs that are too often equated with wants. The Scriptures identify a "common good" in 1 Corinthians 12:7: "To each is given the manifestation of the Spirit for the common good." Spiritual gifts and disposition are given for the corporate upbuilding of Christ's church and for its mission in the world. The loss of the common good is a matter for concern. Development of a communitarian agenda requires an emphasis on the common good. In this area, Christians in the United States can learn much from churches in Asia, Africa, and Latin America.[31] In such settings, a commitment to the corporate good transcends the priority of an individual resulting in the development of a communal identity and a sense of global mission.

In his thinking about education, Gene Getz made explicit the importance of edification in addition to evangelism. He based his thoughts on the educational commission of Matthew's Gospel that stresses the making of disciples (Matt. 28:18–20).[32] For edification to function in relation to the cooking metaphor requires the vulnerability of all participants to become more than any one person through interaction. This does not suggest loss of personal identity, but rather sharing that identity openly with others in the common pot or venture. Openness to others enables the possibility of transformation and liberation through identification and ownership of God's larger purposes for the community and wider society.[33] This calls for full partnership with the Trinity extending into the life of the faith community that dares to discern God's will. The discernment of God's will requires confirmation of what the Spirit is suggesting through multiple witnesses and, wherever possible, a working for consensus. When consensus is not possible, a trust in appointed or emergent leadership may be required. In many settings, heeding the voices of those who have been marginalized from the particular community is essential to gain perspective. The struggle with discerning corporate direction may increasingly involve conflict and require creative strategies for resolving conflict. When things do heat up, as typifies most cooking processes, the perspective of Philippians 2:3–5 applies: "Do nothing from selfish ambition or conceit, but in humility regard others as better than yourselves. Let each of you look not to your own interests, but to the interests of others. Let the same mind be in you that was in Christ Jesus." With the focus on Jesus, the perspective of his second coming provides insights for the place of glorification.

Glorification—Took

The realities of glorification as they relate to eschatology is the focus of chapter 6. The connection to note here is that the present sense of future salvific blessings in Jesus Christ provides perspective on what participants are expected to take with them from any educational encounter. Ultimately, the category *took* considers what persons will take with them into eternity. I recall a saying from my initial ventures into Christian discipleship as a young adult: "Only one life, 'twill soon be past, only what's done for Christ will last." The *took* of any Christian teaching can be evaluated in terms of eternal or kingdom values. The refinement of faith and the experience of salvation have a goal in mind that is described in 1 John 3:2–3: "Beloved, we are God's children now; what we will be has not yet been revealed. What we do know is this: when he is revealed, we will be like him, for we will see him as he is. And all who have this hope in him purify themselves, just as he is pure." This passage combines the paradoxical realities of revelation and mystery. Mystery resides in what has not yet been revealed. Revelation is discovered in the face-to-face encounter with Jesus and seeing him as he is. This is a source of wonder and awe. It is also a call to accountability and commitment. The Christian hope of glorification is a motivation for righteous living. For Christian teaching, this implies encouragement for participants to live in the light of new truth discovered or revealed. More than encouragement, participants are challenged to act with the identification of avenues for accountability before God and others. Christian truth is finding expression in life and bringing glory to the name of Jesus Christ. To be like Jesus at his glorious appearing motivates teachers and students alike in godly living. The Apostle Paul acknowledges this dynamic of teachers serving as models and mentors to others just as Jesus discipled his followers: "Be imitators of me, as I am of Christ" (1 Cor. 11:1). The imitation of Christ as seen in the life and teaching of Christian educators is what students can take with them into the world. Paul's use of the word *as* is an important qualifier, for the extent to which Christ is discerned in the teacher determines the ultimate worth of imitation. This places a greater obligation upon teachers as James 3:1 suggests: "Not many of you should become teachers, my brothers and sisters, for you know that we who teach will be judged with greater strictness." In the following verses of James 3, the writer warns of the importance of taming the tongue and the distinction between two forms of wisdom. The wisdom that can spring forth from the sanctified speech of teachers is "peaceable, gentle, willing to yield, full of mercy and good fruits, without a trace of partiality or hypocrisy" (v. 17). These characteristics are possible for the focus of any *took* proposed for teaching. They suggest eternal values that bring glory to God and are embraced in the glorification of Christian believers.

The Question of Conversion and Transformation

The exploration of salvation is incomplete without a consideration of conversion or transformation. Christian educators have connected these terms to teaching. Though conversion traditionally has been associated with justification, I have elsewhere suggested that conversion has wider implications for the ongoing processes of sanctification and edification in a fuller understanding of trinitarian grammar.[34] Transformation is a term that both religious and general educators have applied to their teaching in the hope of fostering change. In referring to transformative education, I maintain that Christian educators need to return to the Scriptures and to make explicit the theological connection with conversion. The discussion of salvation in this chapter proposes the more specific salvific terms as compared with conversion. The terms related to salvation that emerge from theological sources elaborate upon the more general discussion of conversion and transformation in Christian education. Conversion and transformation assume an ongoing openness to the gracious working of the Holy Spirit in applying the fruits of Christ's ministry to our personal and corporate lives. The application begins with prevenient grace and continues through the experiences of justification, sanctification, edification, and finally glorification. God's full-orbed salvation is a wonder to behold and embrace across the life span from new birth to resurrection.

Conclusion

God works *despite* our sin to offer salvation to humanity. Therefore, the essential teaching of this chapter affirms the following: *Despite* us, God works to transform the sin that besets us through the offer of salvation that we teach. Christian teaching takes seriously the matter of sin and its extent in personal and corporate life. Christian teaching also celebrates the salvation God offers in Jesus Christ and all the blessings that flow from the incarnation. These blessings are the topic of chapter 3 as we consider all that the incarnation of Jesus Christ means for the ministries of teaching.

THREE

GOD WITH US: JESUS, THE MASTER TEACHER

God's remedy for the human condition of sin described in chapter 2 is the coming of the Son. God's Son appears in the person of Jesus Christ, known as Emmanuel or "God *with* us" (Matt. 1:23). The incarnation of God's Son has implications for the practice of education as we seek to draw upon the New Testament example of Jesus as teacher and as we seek an understanding of his person.[1] A fascination with Jesus as teacher has persisted down through the ages and rightfully so. The Jewish leader and teacher Nicodemus expressed this fascination when he encountered Jesus at night. In this encounter Nicodemus first says, "Rabbi, we know that you are a teacher who has come from God; for no one can do these signs that you do apart from the presence of God" (John 3:2). If we are truly committed to the ministries of Christian education, a teacher coming from God demands our attention, wonder, and awe. Those who have given careful attention to the principles and particulars of Jesus' teaching have often responded with hearts and minds pregnant with wonder and awe.[2] For Christians, Jesus alone stands as the Master Teacher, as the exemplar or model for teaching whose life and ministry are worthy of passionate consideration and emulation.

This third chapter will explore how Jesus was, is, and forever will be the Master Teacher. The framework analyzing Jesus' teaching is one that also serves to examine education itself. I define education as the process of sharing content with persons in the context of their communities and societies.[3] This definition identifies an educational trinity of *content, context,* and *persons* that can serve to appreciate the teaching ministry of the Second Person of the divine Trinity, Jesus the Christ. A trinitarian form of analysis follows from proposing the Trinity as an organizing theological theme for Christian education in chapter 1. Jesus as the beloved Son of God filled with the Holy Spirit provides a masterful model for Christian teachers in every age and setting. By studying the *content, context,* and *persons* of Jesus' teaching, Christians have a standard by which to prepare, implement, and evaluate Christian education in its various forms. In this chapter I propose viewing Jesus as the master of the *context* of teaching, the master of the *content* of teaching, and the master of the *persons* of teaching. Anything less than this fails to do justice to the witness of the Christian church through the first two millennia and the continued relevance of Jesus' model for present and future teachers. Jesus as the Master Teacher incarnates the ideal for an effective educator. Gabriel Moran suggests "to teach is to show someone how to live and how to die."[4] Jesus of Nazareth most wondrously models living and dying for all of humanity.

Jesus is unique as a teacher because he is the very Son of God and is also fully human. The christological formulations of the Council of Chalcedon in the fifth century sought to capture this uniqueness by stating that Jesus is both fully God and fully human—one person with two distinct natures. In Christ's person, the divine maintains priority over the human. James Loder and Richard Osmer point out the significance of the Chalcedonian form and grammar for Christian education theory and practice. Osmer notes that "the grammar consists of three rules that characterize the relationship between the human and divine in Jesus Christ: indissoluble differentiation, inseparable unity, and indestructible order."[5] The bipolar unity between theology and other forms of inquiry gives priority to theological insights and seeks to transform knowledge from sources other than God's special revelation in order to acquire wisdom.[6] In considering the incarnation of Jesus Christ, teachers like Nicodemus recognize that he is a teacher who has come from God calling for our attentive study. With the writer to the Colossians, we note that in Christ "are hidden all the treasures of wisdom and knowledge" (Col. 2:3). Peter Hodgson affirms this perennial truth in his comments on the significance of Jesus' earthly teaching for education today:

> *Christian* theology of education takes its orientation on the paradigmatic figure of Jesus of Nazareth, who incarnates God's Wisdom in his teaching and practice, his way of living and dying. The central image of his teaching was that of a new and radically open community of freedom in which God's Wisdom prevails as opposed to the foolishness and weakness of human wisdom. This divine Wisdom overthrows the dominant logic of the world (hierarchical, authoritarian, juridical, dualistic) in favor of a new logic, that of grace, love, freedom, of uncoerced and fully reciprocal communicative practices.[7]

Hodgson's comments raise a number of questions for how Jesus' teaching relates to the practice of both Christian and general education.

The educational trinity form that I use in this chapter affirms the primary connection of Jesus' teaching with his divinity, whereas the five-task model discussed in other portions of this work affirms the connection with humanity as the church of Christ lives out its calling in the world. Both are rooted in the life and ministry of Jesus the Christ. The Chalcedonian form that emerged from historical discussions of Jesus holds Jesus' divinity and humanity in a creative and dynamic relationship of differentiation, unity, and order. The order modeled by Jesus is the order of loves as stated in the two great commandments of loving God and others.

In Jesus, Christian educators also discover the incarnation of organizing principles for teaching. The two principles I identify in *Principles and Practices of Christian Education* are those of conversion or transformation and connection.[8] Christians claim that transformation with Jesus Christ in his earthly ministry is now possible through the ministry of the Holy Spirit. This transformation makes possible a connection with the Trinity in human life that in turn affects all of creation. A third principle that emerges from my present consideration of Jesus is the Galilean principle. This third principle complements the principles of conversion and connection and is implicit in Jesus' incarnation. The Galilean principle calls for huddling that recognizes and honors differences and for mixing that affirms a greater unity along the various dimensions of educational practice that will be explored in chapter 6. The Galilean principle honors the perspective of those who are marginalized and those who identify with the marginalized. Christian teachers are called to care for those considered as "other" and to recognize the "other" that resides in each of us. In the faces of those in need, we see Jesus, as the writer of Matthew's Gospel suggests in Matthew 25:31–46.

Questions for Consideration

Readers should consider several questions as they explore the model of Jesus' teaching presented in this chapter. These questions can guide discussion and include the following:

How can we be like Jesus in our teaching?[9]

Why not be like Jesus in our teaching?

In what areas should we not strive to emulate or model Jesus in our teaching and why?

How is Jesus' teaching distinctive in relation to the particular context, content, and persons of his first-century encounters and his unique calling as God's Son?

What limitations prevent our teaching practices from being like those of Jesus?

What additional resources are available to us that were not at Jesus' disposal?

How do God's perennial purposes as exemplified in Jesus transcend the first-century to guide contemporary teaching efforts?

With whom might we share what we learn about Jesus'
model of teaching?

What can we do differently in our teaching today to better
reflect the power and relevance of Jesus' model?

Where is God calling us to make a difference through our
teaching?

How might we be more responsive to Christ's Spirit in our
teaching and in empowering the teaching of others?

Who is God calling us to be as teachers in the light of Jesus'
example?

In posing these and other questions, we are following the
model of Jesus, who effectively used questions to raise persons'
spiritual awareness and to offer the possibility of transformative
and anointed teaching. Jesus' use of questions is a result of his
sensitivity to the context of his teaching—first-century Palestine that was subject to Roman domination and cultural cross-
currents (Luke 2:1–4).

The Context of Jesus' Teaching

The world in which Jesus taught has been the subject of
scholarly scrutiny in an effort to gain perspective on his mas-
tery of ministry. First-century Palestine stood at the crossroads
of various teaching traditions that were present in Hellenistic
culture under Roman rule. Palestine was influenced by the traditions of Egypt, Babylon, Syria, Assyria, Greece, Rome, and
preeminently Israel. As a Jew, Jesus grew and matured in a
diverse and multicultural context. It is likely that Jesus himself
was trilingual, speaking Aramaic in everyday conversation,
Hebrew in the local synagogue, and Greek in his carpentry pro-
fession. His lingual and cultural fluency served to enrich his
teaching repertoire. Despite these diverse traditions, we recognize that Jesus primarily drew upon his Jewish tradition in
teaching and was even recognized by Nicodemus, a Jewish
authority, as a rabbi (John 3:2).

Consideration of the tradition one draws from in teaching is important because of how education serves to pass on traditions to others. Persons may reshape and reform traditions in teaching just as Jesus did in relation to the Jewish tradition.[10] While Jesus' teaching ministry was primarily to the house of Israel, he from the time of his birth interacted with diverse cultural groups and even commended the faith of those who were Gentiles (Matt. 2:1–11; 8:28–34; Mark 7:24–30; Luke 7:1–7; 10:25–37; 17:11–19; John 4:1–26; 12:20–26). The value of cultural and lingual fluency and the ability to move beyond one's tradition is affirmed by the Apostle Paul as an asset for ministry in 1 Corinthians 9:20: "To the Jews I became as a Jew, in order to win Jews. To those under the law I became as one under the law (though I myself am not under the law) so that I might win those under the law." In addition, at the birth of the Christian church in Acts 2, the impact of the preaching and teaching was extended as persons heard the gospel in their own languages.

Teaching holds potential for assisting others to explore the points of continuity and change in their traditions. It also provides the opportunity to consider what new things God may be doing in our lives and our receptivity to those divine gifts (Matt. 13:52). The promise of Christ's Spirit to his disciples identifies these two dimensions of the teaching ministry. In John 14:26 Jesus tells his disciples, "But the Advocate, the Holy Spirit, whom the Father will send in my name, will teach you everything, and remind you of all that I have said to you." This is the promise of continuity in relation to the teaching and tradition of Jesus. However, in John 16:12–13 additional insights are shared: "I still have many things to say to you, but you cannot bear them now. When the Spirit of truth comes, he will . . . speak whatever he hears, and he will declare to you the things that are to come." This represents a promise of change and new possibilities in Jesus' teaching and, I suggest, in our teaching as well.

In studying Jesus' teaching context, it is helpful to consider how he was rabbinic in following his Jewish tradition. However, it is also insightful to consider how Jesus was unrabbinic in moving beyond his Jewish tradition. This movement incarnates the Galilean principle for Christian education.

Jesus: Rabbinic and Unrabbinic

In comparing Jesus' teaching with that of his contemporaries, we discern how he related to the wider context of rabbinic teaching.[11] Robert Stein, in his work *The Method and Message of Jesus' Teachings*, provides a helpful discussion of the ways in which Jesus was both rabbinic and unrabbinic. Jesus was rabbinic in that he proclaimed divine law (Mark 12:28–34); taught in the synagogues (Mark 1:21–28, 39; 3:1–6); gathered disciples in his teaching (Mark 1:16–20; 3:13–19); debated with the scribes (Mark 11:27–33; 12:13–27); was asked to settle legal disputes (Mark 12:13–17); sat as he taught, which was the typical stance (Matt. 5:1; Mark 4:1; 9:35); and supported his teachings with reference to the Scriptures (Mark 2:25–26). In all of these ways, Jesus followed the norms for rabbis as they performed the sacred and worshipful task of imparting wisdom. However, Stein also notes ways in which Jesus was unrabbinic. Jesus taught out of doors (Mark 2:13; 6:32–44). He taught women, tax collectors, sinners, and children (Matt. 11:16–19; Mark 2:14–17; 10:13–16; Luke 7:39). His disciples followed him and not just a tradition (Luke 9:21–27). The disciples' message was of Jesus' person as well as his words (Book of Acts). Jesus was greater than Jonah and Solomon in relation to his wisdom and impact (Matt. 12: 38–42), and he was both a prophet and a teacher (Mark 6:1–6). All of these distinctives set Jesus apart from his contemporaries and resulted in a lasting impact upon all of his followers.[12] Finally, we must also recognize Jesus' unique redemptive mission as the Son of God that serves to distinguish his teaching from that of all others.

What implications can we draw from this comparison of Jesus and his contemporaries? On the one hand, conformity to certain contextual and cultural norms can assure a teacher of an audience that may be initially receptive. The creation of extreme dissonance, contradiction, or conflict may be counterproductive for the learning process. On the other hand, to sustain interest over time requires variety and a certain degree of novelty. Allowing space for creative expression and imaginative play and breaking down oppressive boundaries can lead to transformative teaching and learning as the Spirit of God invites new life to emerge. The challenge for teachers, of course, is to discern when change is needed and when continuity with a tradition holds more potential for transformation as suggested by Chalcedonian grammar or form.[13] The distinctive calling of teachers is to provide access to the intellectual and formative traditions of a culture with the hope that these traditions themselves foster renewal and change where needed. For this transformation to occur, teachers need to clearly explain the possibilities for change and growth. They need to invite students to discover such possibilities for themselves. Such a task is riddled with risks that are well worth taking. In the case of Jesus, the risks involved rejection, betrayal, and denial at the hands of his own followers.

For teachers to foster both continuity and change in the cultural passage of generations requires a wisdom and grace that God alone can provide. Teachers must discern where their gifts and callings fit into and transcend their cultural landscapes just as Jesus did in his first-century context. The wrestling with and discernment of truth through others is a lifelong task calling for the devotion of teachers and learners alike. Those "others" must include persons who have gone before us and have left heritages or legacies. Such cultural legacies represent the roots of a tree that must be tended lest the tree lose access to the required nutrients in the common soil. Once rooted in a tradition, that tree can branch out in new and unexpected ways. Those branches can then set the platform from which new educational wings are tested. Certainly, Jesus affirmed the place of traditions that offered new life to his followers. However, he denounced those traditions that squelched the life of those most needing support. Jesus brought new life to the rabbinic tradition by embodying an expression of teaching that was distinctive and faithful to the spirit of Judaism. He broke out of boundaries that prevented persons like women, children, sinners, and Gentiles from experiencing the new life offered by God. Jesus compelled persons to become all God intended them to be. Those who sat at his feet and listened with open hearts discovered that new life in the cultural backwaters of Galilee. "Can anything good come from Galilee?" Jesus' followers were asked. What could someone from Nazareth offer to the culturally sophisticated of first-century Palestine?

Galilee: A Multicultural Setting

Recent scholarship has emphasized the multicultural context of Galilee. Galilee was a region comprised of Gentiles and foreigners, of people from various nations. It was a region that was constantly experiencing infiltration and migration. At various times in its history, Galilee was controlled by Babylon, Persia, Macedonia, Egypt, Syria, and Assyria. In the first century, Galilee had a population of approximately 350,000 persons, including a large slave element and about 100,000 Hellenized Jews. The primary language at this time was Koine Greek, although Jews spoke Aramaic. Galilean Jews were lax in the matter of personal attendance at the temple in Jerusalem, in part for the obvious reason of distance. This attitude was symbolic of the modified orthodoxy of Jews in Galilee of the Gentiles. It is significant that much of Jesus' teaching, directed primarily to those living in the Galilean context, was not acceptable to the orthodox interpreters of Judea. He gained a reputation for unusual interpretation. Jesus manifested a freshness and independence of mind as to the meaning and application of the law that was consistent with the spirit of Galilee, a region occupied by a mixed population and having a reputation for racial variety in and around its borders.[14] Its cultural diversity posed a direct challenge to the perceived cultural purity of Judea and Jerusalem. Why would the Son of God choose to be incarnated in and identified with such a setting? What does commitment to and engagement in a multicultural reality suggest for teaching strategies enamored with homogeneous groupings and a press for cultural conformity?

The motley collection of Jesus' twelve apostles may also confound the usual recruitment strategies for Christian discipleship efforts. How did Jesus function in such a context? The Gospel of John gives us insights regarding how Jesus responded to the contextual realities of his association with Galilee. In John 1:43–51 we find the account of Jesus calling Nathaniel and Philip. Philip's witness to the person of Jesus in verse 45 is, "We have found him about whom Moses in the law and also the prophets wrote, Jesus son of Joseph from Nazareth." The mention of Nazareth of Galilee concerns Nathaniel to such an extent that he asks, "Can anything good come out of Nazareth?"

Nathaniel's question represents a cultural bias and illustrates the fear of cultural mixing that characterized Nazareth and Galilee. Philip's response to Nathaniel is, "Come and see," which Nathaniel does. Upon encountering Nathaniel, Jesus identifies him as "truly an Israelite in whom there is no deceit!" (v. 47). Nathaniel in turn declares of Jesus, "Rabbi, you are the Son of God! You are the King of Israel!" (v. 49). Nathaniel's transformation from initial misperception and reluctance is remarkable and signals Jesus' openness to those coming with cultural biases and limitations, including all of us. Jesus' person and ministry broke cultural expectations for Nathaniel. Jesus modeled an openness to those on the cultural margins that suggests a need for "mixing" as discussed in chapter 6.[15]

The second passage we find in the seventh chapter of John, with special reference to verses 1–9 and 40–52. Jesus' brothers encouraged him to go publicly to Judea and Jerusalem to reveal himself as the Son of God at the Festival of Booths. The text in verse 5 notes that they did not really believe in Jesus and that Jesus himself knew of a plot by some of the hate-filled Jewish leaders to kill him. Jesus initially opts to remain in the safe setting of Galilee. However, after his brothers leave, Jesus decides to go to Jerusalem in secret, without the public and provocative display they suggested. About the middle of the festival, Jesus does publicly teach in the temple. He carefully weighs the risks and assesses the situation on site. The truth and offer of living water in his teaching results in a division among his hearers that is apparent in verses 40–52, where his association with Galilee is problematic for both the crowd and the Jewish leaders.

This second passage from John 7 poses questions of cultural boundaries and the differences between cultural insiders and outsiders in teaching. Confronting outsiders invites the possibility of transformation as suggested by Chalcedonian grammar and the ministry of the Holy Spirit. Those from Judea and the leadership in Jerusalem were the cultural insiders, and those associated with Galilee, including Jesus, were the cultural outsiders. Despite being viewed as an outsider, Jesus considered the risks and opted to share wisdom and truth even with those who hated or rejected him. The role of Nicodemus is also noteworthy. In John 3 Nicodemus, a cultural insider, comes to Jesus at night, possibly to avoid observation by others. However, here in chapter 7 he is willing to be a reluctant advocate for Jesus to the extent of being identified as a Galilean himself. Nicodemus spoke up in a group that had a definite contempt for Galilee. He wanted others to hear Jesus out and to carefully consider what Jesus was doing before judging him.

One implication for teaching is the need for a safe place to explore the truth and openness to cultural and ethnic diversity as modeled for us by Jesus' ministry in Galilee.[16] Multicultural education is an area of need among Christians committed to educating the whole people of God. Multicultural education suggests a concern with creating educational environments in which participants from all cultural groups will experience educational equity.[17] For me, "educational equity" can be defined in terms of access to educational resources, respect of differences, space to be heard, appropriate role models, and shared power to make educational decisions. Jesus did not experience this equity in being identified as a Galilean in John 7, despite his birth in Bethlehem of Judea. Nicodemus acted as an advocate for this equity before the chief priests and his fellow Pharisees, the cultural insiders. Jesus incarnated the Galilean principle in his teaching.

Jesus' Distinctives in His Context

How did Jesus stand out in his first century context? As a teacher sent from God, what distinctives characterize Jesus? For me these distinctives can be associated with the threefold office historically identified with Jesus' person and ministry as it reflects the ministry of the Trinity: prophet, priest, and king. These three roles can be restated to include the prophetic, pastoral, and political dimensions of Jesus' teaching. Jesus' teaching was prophetic in the sense of sharing God's truth that breaks through tradition to reappropriate spirit and life. The norms and forms of personal and common life in first-century Palestine squelched the full possibilities of God's intentions for Israel and all nations, requiring the new agenda embodied in Jesus the Christ. Jesus' teaching explored the new terms of God's provision as made possible in his very life, death, and resurrection.

The fullness of time had come according to God's plan, and Jesus offered a new choice to fulfill divine intentions for the creation. Jesus the prophet encouraged persons to choose life offered now in him.

Jesus' teaching was pastoral in the sense of knowing the human heart and ministering to our deepest needs with healing and wholeness. This healing and wholeness are related to the experience of salvation that includes justification for one's sins in receiving God's indescribable gift of Jesus Christ (2 Cor. 9:15); the process of sanctification throughout one's journey in experiencing God's holiness in all aspects of life; the mutual ministry of edification in the Christian church in its gathered and scattered expressions; and the hope of our final glorification and full adoption as God's children at the consummation (Rom. 8:28–30).

While we name and celebrate these distinctives in Jesus, we must also recognize the reception he received in his setting. How did his politics play out? Jesus as a teacher had to contend with an unwelcome reception by many to what he was proclaiming. In another work, I identified four realities of this reception. The facts of Jesus' incarnation, the threat to his life in Bethlehem, his rejection in his hometown of Nazareth, and his crucifixion in Jerusalem all point to the risks and costs of teaching the truth in his time and the political dimensions of his ministry.[18] In understanding these particulars, teachers become aware of the present risks and costs of teaching. Beyond consideration of the *context* of Jesus' teaching that sets the stage and serves to identify the Galilean principle for Christian education, Christians must also examine the *content* of his masterful example.

The Content of Jesus' Teaching

One classic study of Jesus as teacher is the work of educator Herman Horne (1874–1946), who taught for many years at New York University. Horne's work was originally titled *Jesus: The Master Teacher*, the same title of this chapter, and was republished in 1971 as *Teaching Techniques of Jesus*. In its current incarnation, the title is *Jesus the Teacher: Examining His Expertise in Edu-*

cation.[19] A summary of this work is worth quoting at length to introduce the content and methods of Jesus' teaching:

> The teaching situation is complex, though it may easily be resolved into its essential elements: teacher, student, lesson, aim of the teacher, method of teaching, and environment.
>
> The conversation of Jesus with the woman of Samaria is an object lesson in teaching in all these respects.
>
> Jesus began by winning attention through openers that centered students' interests; then he established some point of contact with his hearers on the physical or spiritual plane.
>
> As a teacher, he was not only a tactician with methods but also a strategist with objectives. His greatest objective was to share with people that sense of union with the Father that he enjoyed.
>
> Jesus based his teaching on the vital problems in the lives of his students.
>
> Though he was not a Greek, he was ready to converse in a profitable way as was Socrates, and he led a more public life, though shorter, than did Socrates.
>
> He asked and answered questions to stimulate self-expression, desiring conviction rather than persuasion on the part of his followers. His questions are better than those of Socrates because they are mostly of a kind other than leading.
>
> He used discourse at many different times before many different groups on many different themes, but always in a more or less informal way.
>
> He told stories with a point, the parables, which his listeners did not always understand but which always made them think and led the spiritually minded to inquire into their meaning.
>
> He knew and used the Old Testament Scriptures, both for the needs of his own soul and as a common meeting ground with the religious minds of his day.
>
> He never let an occasion slip but utilized it as it arose to clarify thought and to guide life.
>
> The principle of true learning is recognized in his words: "He who has ears, let him hear," and all his parables present the less familiar in terms of the familiar. Even so, he was often misunderstood.
>
> He used the principle of contrast to make real the portrayal of truth, concrete examples to bring the abstract near, symbols to make, if possible, difficult meanings plain, and wonderful

imagery to enhance the appeal to the imagination and so to lead people to conviction.

He cared more for individuals than for crowds, though he would often minister to crowds, perhaps with a view to reaching individuals.

He trained his disciples as witnesses of him, by personal association, individualizing instruction, and meeting the needs of each one.

The work accomplished by Jesus and through others, under his tutelage, was based on high motivation because of the awakening spiritual and altruistic impulses rather than those of personal advancement.

In a most interesting way, Jesus probed the depths of human nature and touched on most of the innate reactions of man, though some, like rivalry, he did not conspicuously appeal to, and some, like sex, he sublimated.

All the methods of impression he used were but means to expression. Jesus was far more pragmatic than either idealistic or mystic.

Jesus appreciated childhood and made its characteristics identical with those of membership in the kingdom.

In a way not surprising but confirming our previous impressions, Jesus embodies those qualities of the teacher commonly set up as ideal.

As we followed these discussions we doubtless discovered repeatedly that the problems of teaching that we ourselves face are similar to those that Jesus faced and that the solutions he found will greatly assist us in our work.

Jesus is the master teacher. Have we made him ours?[20]

Horne's insights emphasize Jesus' distinctive ways of teaching that enabled his students, the disciples, to recall lessons that were never written down by Jesus himself.

Principles of Jesus' Teaching

From Horne's account it is possible to identify five principles of Jesus' teaching practice:

1. *Jesus' teaching was authoritative.*[21] Jesus taught as one who had authority (Mark 1:14–15, 21–22), demonstrated by

his actions and words. This authority was authenticated in terms of his content and his person. The content of his teaching was the revelation of God, for he spoke with the words of God the Father (John 14:23–24). In addition, Jesus' life and ministry authenticated his authority.

2. *Jesus' teaching was not authoritarian.* While being authoritative, Jesus' teaching was not forced or imposed upon his hearers, as evidenced in John 6:60–69. Jesus specified the costs and demands of discipleship and encouraged his followers to make personal commitments of their choosing.

3. *Jesus' teaching encouraged persons to think.* Jesus stimulated serious thought and questioning in his teaching, and he expected his hearers to carefully consider their responses to the truths he shared. He did not provide a simple, ready-made answer to every problem of life. Rather, Jesus expected his students to search their minds and hearts in relation to his teachings and to consider the realities of life. In encouraging others to think for themselves, Jesus posed questions and allowed for questioning.

4. *Jesus lived what he taught.* Jesus faithfully incarnated his message through his life and ministry. Before commanding his disciples to serve and love one another as he had loved them (John 13:12–17, 34–35), Jesus demonstrated the full extent of his love by washing their feet. He then further demonstrated his love by laying down his life for his friends, his brothers and sisters (John 15:12–13).

5. *Jesus loved those he taught.* Jesus loved his students in a way that indicates the deep longings of every heart for an intimate relationship with another person and with God. This relationship of love with Jesus was also characterized by an equal concern for truth as the Master Teacher communicated it.[22]

These principles operate in the variety of teachings that Jesus shared as recorded in the Gospels.

Jesus' Teaching in the Gospels

Each Gospel writer provides a distinct portrayal of Jesus as teacher, and this variety is fascinating. In Matthew's Gospel, Jesus is portrayed as a masterfully prepared educator whose teaching is summarized in five blocks of teaching that include the three elements of memory (or history), vision, and mission for the Christian community. The five blocks are organized in the following way:

5:1–7:27	a vision for participation in God's kingdom
10:1–42	mission directives for the disciples
13:1–52	an outline of redemptive history
18:1–35	the mission of discipline in a local body of disciples that calls for love, healing, reconciliation, and justice
23:1–25:46	a vision for God's future kingdom with Jesus' teaching on eschatology, the study of end times[23]

Mark's Gospel portrays Jesus as a teacher of authority and action who makes a difference in individual lives and in the wider community. Luke's Gospel portrays Jesus as the inclusive and welcoming teacher who honors women, children, sinners, and even Gentiles in his outreach. John's Gospel portrays Jesus as the personal and intimate teacher who knows the hearts and minds of each of his followers and establishes a special relationship with every person who is open and vulnerable to him. While there are other characteristics of Jesus' teaching content that could be analyzed, his major theme is the kingdom of God as it breaks into human society and individual lives through his very person. This revolutionary and potentially transformative theme is at the core of Jesus' educational ministry and provides unity within the variety of his teaching.

Two themes of Jesus' teaching in the Gospels have been explored in recent educational discussions. The first theme is the kingdom or reign of God that has been proposed as a paradigm for Christian education.[24] In my own writing, I have maintained that Christian education is a preparadigmatic discipline.

Various approaches to Christian education need to be supported rather than one dominant paradigm to encompass *all* the diversity we encounter in human creation and education.[25] At the same time, I identified contours of an emerging paradigm because of my experiences in Latin America.[26] While this may present a paradox, I maintain that the study and discovery of God assumes the place of mystery as well as revelation.

The *mysterium tremendum* reminds us of the unconditional dimensions of life and warns us of the potential idolatry of any one paradigm that seeks to reinvent the tower of Babel. Christians are called to recognize the place of no-knowledge, the null curriculum, and excluded knowledge in any one dominant paradigm that might be proposed. The greater concern is to honor various voices, recognize certain values or virtues as universal, and acknowledge that we cannot fathom the depth and mystery of God in any one paradigm. Does loving God with all of our minds assume the imposition of one dominant paradigm? Not if we honestly recognize our limitations. Imposing one metatheory or paradigm may foreclose the search for truth and the honoring of distinct voices from those on the margins.[27] Such a search too often ends prematurely, squelching our encounters with the awesome God who breaks all of our categories and delights to dwell in the surprises of life as typified in Jesus' teaching ministry.

God is a consuming fire; the Spirit is likened to the wind whose directions cannot be determined; and Jesus offers the living water that is dynamic and unpredictable in its movements. I have opted for the Trinity as an organizing theme rather than the reign of God as a paradigm. The Trinity assumes plurality as well as unity. The search for one paradigm honors the need for control, order, and form. For me that needs to be balanced with a concern for surrender, ardor, and freedom that I believe is found in the life of the Trinity. My advocacy can be compared with an essay written by Isaiah Berlin that compares a fox and a hedgehog.[28] In Berlin's thought the hedgehog knows how to do one thing very well—dig holes.[29] By comparison, the fox knows how to do a variety of things depending upon the situation. By not embracing one dominant paradigm, I suggest the need for a foxlike approach rather than a hedgehog approach.

Paradigms are too often maintained in a way that limits inquiry, open-ended dialogue, and creativity. In the pursuit of unity, too often uniformity is the result. I affirm the proposal of models and approaches that are shared and subject to wide dialogue and consideration.

The second theme of Jesus' teaching is reconciliation. This theme is identified in chapter 2 and will only be noted here. Jesus worked for reconciliation in his teaching ministry, and his commission to make disciples calls for extensive effort to reconcile persons with God and with each other despite the various lines that divide humanity. This side of eternity, estrangement persists while the ministry of reconciliation proceeds. Paul elaborates on this ministry of reconciliation in 2 Corinthians 5:11–21. While his insights on reconciliation can be used to connect Christian education thought and practice, I prefer to return to the Trinity as a theological organizing theme that provides a dynamic and diverse theological seedbed. A consideration of the values in Jesus' teaching helps us to see possible connections across the theological themes of the reign of God, reconciliation, and the Trinity.

Values in Jesus' Teaching

Beyond the specifics of Jesus' teaching, it is possible to identify the underlying values or virtues it embodies. This is particularly important in a time when values and character formation are priorities in educational forums. In my discussion of Christian values related to teaching in *Basics of Teaching for Christians*, I propose five Christian core values, each with a corresponding call related to teaching. The five values and their related calls are *truth*—a call for integrity; *love*—a call for care; *faith*—a call for action; *hope*—a call for courage; and *joy*—a call for celebration. In that work, I also relate each of these five core values to the five tasks or purposes of the church: proclamation, community formation, service, advocacy, and worship.[30] What is not explicit in that work is how in his teaching Jesus himself embodies each of the values that fulfill God's purposes for all of humanity.

First, in relation to truth, John declares that "the Word became flesh and lived among us, and we have seen his glory, the glory as of a father's only son, full of grace and truth" (John 1:14) and again, "Grace and truth came through Jesus Christ" (John 1:17). Jesus himself definitively claims to be "the way, and the truth, and the life" (John 14:6) and to offer the bread and water of life to his followers (John 4:10, 14; 6:35, 48, 51). In proclaiming and embodying the truth, Jesus offers a model of integrity with a consistency between his words and actions. This consistency validates his message and his worthiness to serve as a model in teaching.

Second, Jesus is a model for the expression of Christian love in how he cared for all those he met. That love included confronting others in their sinful patterns and proposing alternatives. His love also included the supreme gift of laying down his life for his friends (John 15:13) that made possible salvation (John 3:16). His love was demonstrated in the washing of his disciples' feet (John 13:1–20) as he did this while being their "Teacher and Lord" (v. 13). His love involved his willingness to weep for others in their pain and suffering (John 11:35–36) and to rejoice in life's events such as a wedding (John 2:1–11).

Third, Jesus is a model for faith or faithfulness in his actions as a teacher. In *Basics of Teaching for Christians,* I elaborate on these actions. They can be explored here in relation to the eight skills that Joel Davitz identified as typifying effective or faithful teaching. Those eight skills and corresponding examples from Jesus' teaching are: clarity of communication (Mark 1:21–22); use of a variety of teaching methods (Matt. 5:13–16; 6:22; 7:9–11; 10:16; 23:23–24; Mark 8:27–32; 10:24–25; 14:58; Luke 12:16–20; 14:11, 26; 16:10; 19:1–6); enthusiasm (John 2, 3); a task orientation (Matt. 10:1–42); student involvement (John 6:60–69); a varied level of discourse; use of appropriate praise and criticism (Matt. 16:17, 23); and the capacity for self-analysis (Matt. 26:39).[31]

Fourth, Jesus models the value of hope in his courage to confront the human situation with all of its sin and suffering. His message of hope sounded forth in his teaching at the synagogue in Nazareth. As a prophet he was not accepted in his hometown (Luke 4:24), but his message was clear: "The Spirit of the Lord is upon me, because he has anointed me to bring good news to the poor. He has sent me to proclaim release to the captives and recovery of sight to the blind, to let the oppressed go free, to proclaim the year of the Lord's favor" (Luke 4:18–19). This message was fulfilled in Jesus' prophetic actions that brought to fruition God's plan for a renewed humanity and creation. Jesus offers a living hope and transformative possibilities for education and all of life.[32]

Fifth, Jesus models the value of joy in his teaching. This joy is sounded at his birth in the message of the angels and shepherds (Luke 2:10, 20) and in the words of Simeon and Anna as he is presented at the temple (Luke 2:28–32, 38). Jesus' very presence results in joy as persons recognize him and praise God. The same note of joy is sounded at the close of Jesus' earthly ministry as his disciples grasp the significance of his death and resurrection. The disciples on the road to Emmaus, who likely included Cleopas and Mary,[33] along with the eleven and their companions back in Jerusalem, experienced this joy in understanding the significance of Jesus' teaching and ministry for them (Luke 24:13–49). The word used to describe the opening of the Scriptures to Jesus' disciples and the opening of their eyes and minds in Luke 24:31, 32, and 45, is the same word used to describe the opening of a womb at the birth of a child. I came to fully appreciate this joy only by being the coach for my wife at the birth of our daughter. This is the joy that Jesus identifies and prays for in John's Gospel (John 15:11; 16:20–24; 17:13). His relating it to childbirth indicates Jesus' great interest in persons from the very beginning of life to the passing from life to death. Jesus' attention to persons calls for careful consideration of the place, value, and role of persons in his teaching.

The Persons of Jesus' Teaching

In considering the *persons* of teaching, the person of Jesus himself demands immediate attention. As suggested above, the Christian values of *truth, love, faith, hope,* and *joy* find their fullest expression in the life and ministry of Jesus. He embodies the quintessential ideal of a teacher who cared deeply for all the persons he encountered, including those who desired his death. He cared enough about his enemies to share the truth and to consider the heart matters at the center of their opposition. He knew the deepest longings of the human heart and the genuine questions of the human mind, and he shared his teaching in ways that invited transformation. He also cared enough about persons to allow them to wrestle with alternatives and to decide for themselves about the direction of their personal and corporate lives. He valued persons as created by God and having infinite value and worth. Because of their role as creatures, he also held persons accountable before God for the choices they made and their responses to the human situation of sin and suffering. Given the choices before persons, Jesus persistently upheld others in prayer so that spiritual resources might sustain them. Jesus' prayer life also sustained him in the demands of his teaching ministry. Christian educators today can be encouraged to follow Jesus' example as they regularly speak to God about their teaching relationships. Jesus' teaching example reveals the underlying Chalcedonian grammar or form of his life and ministry, and it points to the matter of mentoring, a subject of increasing interest in education and related fields.

Jesus as Mentor

In her work *Mentoring in Religious Education*, Leona English draws on a comprehensive definition of mentoring as

> a nurturing process in which a more skilled or more experienced person, serving as a role model, teaches, sponsors, encourages, counsels, and befriends a less skilled or less experienced person for the purpose of promoting the latter's professional and/or personal development. Mentoring functions are carried out within the context of an ongoing, caring relationship between the mentor and protégé.[34]

According to this definition, Jesus was a mentor in his teaching to and with his followers. Robert Kelley, in his work *The Power of Followership*, makes a clear distinction between mentoring and discipling. He suggests that unlike mentoring, "which is an intensive one-on-one experience aimed at personal maturation, discipleship involves a body of knowledge being passed from a teacher to a group of students." For Kelley, discipleship involves embracing a paradigm or a worldview, becoming one of the family, and being at home in a tradition.[35] My own thinking and Jesus' model differ from Kelley's clear demarcations by incorporating both mentoring and discipling. Jesus certainly passed on a new tradition that later emerged as the Christian faith, and he related to his followers as disciples who would continue in his ways. However, Jesus also deeply related to his followers as persons who had distinct personalities, needs, and trajectories for their development.

Jesus' sensitivity to mentoring is clear in the account of John 21 where Peter encounters Jesus after his threefold denial and is restored to relationship. In verses 20–23, Peter compares his future with that of the beloved disciple. Jesus delineates the paths of his followers from each other and maintains their individuality. He respects the person of Peter and that of the beloved disciple, who some have identified as John. Some forms of comparison and competition may be inevitable in a teaching setting, but Jesus modeled a deeper concern for individuals. Jesus made explicit that what God expects of each person may differ. The masterful way in which he attended to each of his disciples is described in the classic work of A. B. Bruce, *The Training of the Twelve*.[36] Jesus had a unique ability to discern the particular needs and struggles of each person he encountered, and he tailored his teaching approach accordingly. For example, his encounter and confrontation with Nicodemus in John 3 differs significantly from his interaction with the Samaritan woman at the well in John 4. His treatment of his enemies differs widely from that of his inner circle with whom he shared the interpretation of his parables.

The classical example of mentoring comes from Homer's epic poem *The Odyssey*, where Mentor is the aged protector of the absent Odysseus's property and family. In particular, Mentor is responsible for the education and guidance of Telemachus, Odysseus's son. In Homer's account, the Greek goddess Athena also takes on the form of Mentor to provide support for both Telemachus and Odysseus. Traits of this classical mentoring relationship include protection, stewardship, education, guidance, advocacy, wisdom, friendship, resourcing, integrity, counsel, encouragement, confirmation, and seasoned reflection. In the fullness of time, God sent his Son in the person of Jesus to fulfill the deep human hunger for a mentor. Jesus was an exemplar in all the classical traits that Homer's epic suggested were essential in life's journey. Jesus' earthly disciples had the privilege of being mentored face-to-face. That mentoring is now extended through the Christian church to current followers of Jesus. The role of Christian teachers today incarnates the mentoring tradition of Jesus.

One way to evaluate the impact of a mentor is to examine the lives and ministries of persons being mentored. Matt Friedeman, in his work *The Master Plan of Teaching*, provides an account of what historical records and church tradition reveal in the case of Jesus' students:

> *Matthew* first taught and wrote in Judea before suffering martyrdom by being slain with a sword in the Ethiopian city of Nadabah.
>
> *John* is thought to have founded the churches of Smyrna, Pergamos, Sardis, Philadelphia, Laodicea, and Thyatira. From Ephesus, he was sent to Rome where he was ordered to be put into a cauldron of boiling oil. He somehow escaped death and was later banished to the Isle of Patmos, the only apostle to escape violent death.
>
> *Peter* ministered in Antioch, Asia Minor, and Rome. He was forced to watch his wife crucified and then he was himself crucified, upside down (at his request) so as not to die as his Lord had died.
>
> *James, son of Zebedee* is said to have brought the Good News of Christ to Spain (today he is their patron saint) and returned later to be beheaded at Jerusalem by King Herod Agrippa I.
>
> *James, son of Alphaeus* was selected to oversee the churches of Jerusalem and was later beaten, stoned, and killed with a fuller's club.
>
> *Philip*, great luminary of Asia, was eventually martyred there by hanging in Hierapolis.

Bartholomew carried the Gospel to several countries and propagated his translation of the Gospel of Matthew in India. He was, according to tradition, arrested, beaten with clubs, flayed alive, and then crucified.

Andrew was a Christian communicator to many lands—Cappadocia, Bithynia, Galatia, Byzantium, and Scythia. In Achaia in Greece, in the town of Patras, Andrew died a martyr, scourged with a rod, fastened to a cross, and left to die.

Thomas went to the Parthians, Medes, Persians, Carmanians, Hyrcanians, Bacatrians, and Magians and eventually died (by the thrust of a spear) in India.

Thaddeus supposedly taught the Gospel in several places and was eventually crucified at Edessa in A.D. 72.

Simon (the Zealot) relayed the Christian message to Mauritania, Africa, and in England where he was crucified.

Matthias (who replaced Judas) was a teacher who for his boldness was stoned and then beheaded in Jerusalem.

While the exact locations and circumstances of the Apostles' deaths may be in dispute, the overwhelming opinion of scholars is that the reproduction of the Christ through their lives was no easy matter. They were forced to give their lives for their faith. Jesus was right. "Wisdom is vindicated by all her children" (Luke 7:35). Justification for the enormous amount of time Jesus invested in these men is found in the spread of the Gospel to "Jerusalem, in all of Judea and Samaria, and even to the remotest part of the earth" (Acts 1:8).[37]

Friedeman's account is a testimony to the impact that Jesus had as a mentor. His life, death, and resurrection transformed the lives of his followers, and his teaching made a difference in the history of humanity. Following Jesus' earthly ministry, his disciples experienced the mentoring of the Holy Spirit whom Jesus himself sent. The Spirit's ministry is the subject of chapter 4. In relation to teaching, Jesus' model demonstrated the priority of relationships for transformation through his mentoring.

The Priority of Relationships

One note that is sounded throughout the Gospel accounts of Jesus' teaching is the importance of persons. The priority of relationships also flows from the organizing theme of the Trinity explored in chapter 1, and Chalcedon provides a structure for relationships. This priority is graphically suggested by the fact that in Jesus, God has taken on human form. Since the incarnation, the understanding of persons best begins with a consideration of Jesus' humanity as a model for all persons. People are indispensable to teaching, though some educational practices appear to ignore them. Teaching brings individuals into relationship. Jesus best demonstrates this principle. We find one striking example of this in John's account of Mary Magdalene's postresurrection encounter with Jesus in the garden.

Some initial comments regarding Mary Magdalene are helpful before turning to John's account because of misunderstanding perpetuated regarding this faithful follower of Jesus. Mary Magdalene was a prominent Galilean woman whom Jesus healed (Mark 16:9; Luke 8:2). She is often misidentified as the harlot from Luke 7:36–50. Mary participated in Jesus' itinerant mission in Galilee and contributed financially to the venture (Mark 15:40–41; Luke 8:1–3). She went with Jesus on his final journey to Jerusalem (Mark 15:41) and was present at the crucifixion (Mark 15:40; John 19:25). She came to the tomb of Joseph of Arimathea to anoint Jesus' body on the first Easter morning (Mark 16:1; Luke 23:55–24:1). Mary reported the fact of the empty tomb and the message of the angels to the eleven disciples (Luke 24:10) and had personal interaction with Jesus after the resurrection as recounted in John 20:11–18.[38] Many have wondered why Mary did not recognize Jesus in this encounter and mistook him for a gardener. However, it is clear to me as a teacher that recognition only came when Jesus called her by name and honored her as a unique person. Mary's response is also significant. Daniel Aleshire comments on this passage: "When Mary is shaken from her false assumption about the individual she is addressing in the garden and recognizes the risen Lord, she calls him

'Teacher' (John 20:16). He had been friend, healer, preacher, prophet, but when she gasps in the reality of his resurrected presence, she claims him as teacher."[39] Once Mary is recognized in her person, she is able to recognize the person of Jesus and his essential role as teacher in her life. This shows the transformative possibility of teaching that honors who others are. In this, Jesus is the stellar example.

Beyond this one example, Jesus' teaching ministry as found in the Gospels repeatedly celebrates his sensitivity to the diverse people he encounters. Of particular note is how he relates to those persons identified as the *anawim*. The *anawim* are those who are poor, humble, and weak before God and others. The *anawim* are those willing to disclose their suffering and open themselves to the redemptive possibilities offered by God. For Christians, the full and final redemptive offering is revealed in the cross of Jesus Christ. The audience for Jesus' teaching included such folk as clearly outlined in Luke 4:18–19. He taught the poor, the captives, the blind, and the oppressed. While these folk may not be a high priority in terms of recruitment efforts for Christian teaching, they were a concern to Jesus. Although the *anawim* represented the marginal groups of society, Jesus frequently used them as valued models of spiritual life instructive to the whole people of God and as evidence of grace extended to all. The New Testament books that best describe Jesus' continuing teaching tradition with the *anawim* are Luke, Acts, and Philemon. In Jesus' earthly ministry, those marginal to society are called to be disciples and to express their discipleship in a variety of ways. For example, Jesus was repeatedly ridiculed for the company he kept—tax collectors, harlots, publicans, and sinners. Yet in his teaching ministry, he preferred to be with these people rather than the recognizably religious. Jesus' intentional plan was to be with those who acknowledged their need of a physician (i.e., the *anawim*).[40] Therefore, Jesus' priority of relationships included those whom others readily sought to avoid. Jesus incarnated the Galilean principle in his teaching by mixing with those on the margins.

Conclusion

By considering the educational trinity of the *context, content,* and *persons* in Jesus' teaching, Christian teachers can gain perspective on their ministries today. Roy Zuck, in his exhaustive work *Teaching as Jesus Taught,* proposes that by examining the effective teaching of Jesus, we can incorporate some of the principles and practices he masterfully modeled. Zuck's list of principles and practices includes the following as we ask ourselves what we might learn about:

Knowing my subject more thoroughly
Knowing my students more intimately
Beginning my lessons more interestingly
Attracting interest more immediately
Aiming my lesson more pointedly
Arousing curiosity more frequently
Motivating my students more actively
Asking questions more provocatively
Answering questions more thoroughly
Lecturing truths more effectively
Telling stories more captivatingly
Presenting Scripture more enthusiastically
Giving facts more picturesquely
Involving students more meaningfully
Quoting Scripture more knowledgeably
Illustrating truths more colorfully
Visualizing concepts more graphically
Applying truths more specifically
Relating truths more personally
Changing lives more deeply
Encouraging students more tenderly
Affirming students more lovingly
Giving counsel more carefully

Correcting students more firmly
Helping students more compassionately
Meeting students more definitely
Testing student learning more accurately
Modeling truth more consistently
Associating with students more informally[41]

Zuck's list applies what is best modeled in Jesus' teaching to those of us who teach today. From the perspective of this chapter, we can celebrate how Jesus was, is, and will continue to be the Master Teacher in relation to the *context, content,* and *persons* of teaching. Jesus, the Master Teacher, continues to inform, form, and transform persons today as in the first century with his presence and power. His presence and power is made available through the person and ministry of the blessed Holy Spirit, which is the focus of chapter 4.

The essential teaching of this chapter is as follows: God *with* us in the person and work of Jesus Christ provides a model for teaching that transcends time. Jesus is a model for all those called to teach, and the incarnation assures Christian teachers that God is with us in the person and ministry of Jesus Christ. By considering Jesus, Christian educators discern both a Chalcedonian form and a Galilean principle to guide their ministries. God with us, made possible through Jesus' coming in the incarnation, makes all the difference. Christians await Christ's second coming, which is the topic of chapter 6. A fitting closure to this chapter are Jesus' parting words to his disciples in Matthew's Gospel and his promise to be with them and us in teaching:

> All authority in heaven and on earth has been given to me. Go therefore and make disciples of all nations, baptizing them in the name of the Father and of the Son and of the Holy Spirit, and teaching them to obey everything that I have commanded you. And remember, I am with you always, to the end of the age. (Matt. 28:18–20)

FOUR

GOD IN US: THE HOLY SPIRIT AND TEACHING

As a blessing of Jesus Christ's work of salvation, Christians experience the indwelling presence of the promised Holy Spirit in their lives. God *in* us through the person and work of the Holy Spirit transforms all dimensions of life, including the ministries of teaching. The indwelling Spirit undergirds the ministry of teaching in its three phases of preparation, instruction, and evaluation.[1] The indwelling Spirit fosters the processes of learning so that the spirits of the students are transformed along with their minds, souls, hearts, and bodies. The mysterious operations of the Spirit are not totally disclosed, nor are they subject to precise human analysis. However, like tracking the winds of climatic changes, persons can inquire about the effects of the Spirit's movements and the nature of the Spirit's partnership in teaching. The author is conscious of the dangers of idolatry and reductionism in any such effort to disclose the Spirit's person and work. Similarly, this reluctance and reverence can limit inquiry about the person and work of both God the Father and God the Son, the other persons of the Trinity. In previous chapters, the entry point for consideration has been biblical revelation or disclosure. Therefore, reference to Scripture takes a priority in exploring the connection between the Holy Spirit and teaching.

In his work *The Logic of the Spirit*, James Loder proposes a Chalcedonian framework for considering the person and work of the Spirit of God.[2] Using this model enables Christian educators to see the work of the Spirit in Jesus' teaching ministry as an entrance for the Spirit's relationship in their own teaching ministry. Loder's work insightfully explores in detail the patterns of human development in relation to the encounter between human spirits and the Holy Spirit. A prior question for me is, how was the Holy Spirit present in the teaching ministry of Jesus?

The Spirit in Jesus' Teaching

From the very conception of Jesus in Mary's womb, the Holy Spirit was present. The angel who appeared to Mary announcing that she would have a child said to her, "The Holy Spirit will come upon you, and the power of the Most High will overshadow you; therefore the child to be born will be holy; he will be called Son of God" (Luke 1:35). Matthew's Gospel notes the fulfillment of the angel's words: "Now the birth of Jesus the Messiah took place in this way. When his mother Mary had been engaged to Joseph, but before they lived together, she was found to be with child from the Holy Spirit" (Matt. 1:18). The role of the Spirit in the conception, development, and birth of persons is essential as the gift of life is shared. The psalmist records the care of God's Spirit from the beginnings of life:

> For it was you who formed my inward parts;
> You knit me together in my mother's womb.
> I praise you, for I am fearfully and wonderfully made.
> Wonderful are your works; that I know very well.
> My frame was not hidden from you,
> When I was being made in secret,
> Intricately woven in the depths of the earth.
> Your eyes beheld my unformed substance.
> In your book were written all the days that were formed for me,
> When none of them as yet existed. (Ps. 139:13–16)

The wonder of God's grace begins with the inception of life in persons who are gifted for the ministries of teaching. As recipients of God's care and gifts, persons share their care for others through teaching and a variety of other ministries. The Spirit bestows gifts as noted: "To each is given the manifestation of the Spirit for the common good" (1 Cor. 12:7). At conception and birth, the Spirit blesses certain individuals with the requisite abilities and gifts to undertake the ministry of teaching for the common good of all. This honors the place of nature in the developmental debate, but does not exclude the importance of nurture or development of the spiritual gifts of teaching. The Spirit interacts with human spirits in the processes of nurture and the unfolding of nature.[3] The potential use of spiritual gifts for teaching depends upon a person's response to God's call and dedicated development of those gifts through training and mutual edification. Training and mutual edification are required to assure "the common good" identified in the Corinthian passage. This was modeled in Jesus' life as he "grew and became strong, filled with wisdom; and the favor of God was upon him" (Luke 2:40).

The Spirit's presence in Jesus' public ministry is also evident in his baptism where "the Holy Spirit descended upon him in bodily form like a dove" (Luke 3:22). After his baptism, when Jesus was "full of the Holy Spirit," (Luke 4:1), "the Spirit immediately drove him out into the wilderness" (Mark 1:12) where he was tempted. With the filling of the Holy Spirit for Jesus' public ministry also come the challenges of opposition and conflict. The Spirit's role in sustaining Jesus through his rigorous wilderness training is evident. In Jesus' initial ministry in Galilee, being "filled with the power of the Spirit, . . . he began to teach in their synagogues and was praised by everyone" (Luke 4:14–15). The reception in his hometown synagogue of Nazareth contrasted with the praiseworthy response in other Galilean towns, but even here Jesus notes the Spirit's presence as he teaches from Isaiah 61:

> The Spirit of the Lord is upon me, because he has anointed me to bring good news to the poor. He has sent me to proclaim release to the captives and recovery of sight to the blind, to let the

oppressed go free, to proclaim the year of the Lord's favor. (Luke 4:18–19)

As he teaches, Jesus applies Isaiah's words to their fulfillment in his own ministry. By teaching in the Spirit, Jesus brings liberation to the lives of his students. The Spirit's anointing of Jesus provides the power to teach, and Jesus' commission from the Father provides the authority to accomplish God's will for those receiving his teaching.[4]

Despite the Spirit's empowerment, the fruits of Jesus' teaching depend upon openness to the Spirit's work in the hearts and lives of his hearers. Jesus' students in Nazareth reject his teaching and resort to violence that does not accomplish its ultimate goal until Jesus' crucifixion. The Spirit's presence and power in the teaching ministry of Jesus suggest the partnership necessary for effective teaching. Nevertheless, even with the Spirit's anointing, opposition and conflict emerge. The results of teaching cannot be guaranteed, as the Spirit must work in those who have ears to hear (Matt. 11:15; 13:9, 43; Mark 4:9, 23; Luke 8:8; 14:35) and spirits responsive to Jesus' gospel teachings. The fruits of teaching are dependent upon the gracious working of God's Spirit to realize learning outcomes. This is the case for Jesus and for all Christian teachers who follow after him. Jesus relied upon the Spirit's power and direction, and his teaching astounded his hearers because "he taught them as one having authority" (Mark 1:22). The Spirit's power and direction are also evident in the Old Testament.

The Spirit in Old Testament Teaching

The Spirit of God is already present in the days of creation. Genesis 1:2 records the following: "Now the earth was formless and empty, darkness was over the surface of the deep, and the Spirit of God was hovering over the waters" (NIV). The Spirit referred to as the wind or breath of life (Gen. 2:7) brings life and order out of the chaos (Isa. 32:15). The teaching ministry seeks to bring a sense of order as well as creative possibilities out of the chaos of lives devoid of God. It does this by sharing the wonders of God's revelation and purposes for all of creation. From the very beginning of life, both order and ardor, form and freedom, discipline and creativity interface. The Spirit of God makes it possible for new life to emerge in creation and in the creative craft of teaching. God's Spirit crafted a new world and invites human participation in procreative acts, including teaching in its varied forms. The Spirit gives life (2 Cor. 3:6) and is life (Rom. 8:10) in the spiritual ministry of teaching. This life-giving ministry stands in contrast to the patterns of death and destruction present in personal and corporate life due to the vast effects of sin as discussed in chapter 2.

One expression of the Spirit's generative work is the giving of prophecy and Scripture. Millard Erickson points out that the "Old Testament prophets testified that their speaking and writing were the result of the Spirit's coming upon them (Ezek. 2:2; 8:3; 11:1, 24; Num. 24:2; 1 Sam. 10:6, 10). . . . Peter confirmed the testimony of the prophets regarding their experience: 'For prophecy never had its origin in the will of man, but men spoke from God as they were carried along by the Holy Spirit' (2 Peter 1:21)."[5] The giving of prophecy and Scripture provides the content for teaching with an added dimension of passion that the prophets included in their communication. The prophetic audience included persons of all nations and social standings. All were called upon to learn the ways of the Lord and were subject to God's standards of righteousness, justice, and peace. Prophetic teaching and writing touched upon all areas of life as God's reign affected all of creation, including the procreation of persons with teaching gifts and abilities.

Erickson points out that an important work of the Holy Spirit in the Old Testament was "conveying certain gifts for various tasks."[6] The first and most striking mention of this work of God's Spirit is found in describing Bezalel's call to build and adorn the tabernacle used in worship: "I have filled him with divine spirit, with ability, intelligence, and knowledge in every kind of craft, to devise artistic designs, to work in gold, silver, and bronze, in cutting stones for setting, and in carving wood, in every kind of craft" (Exod. 31:3–5). The expressive arts are valued as avenues for worship and instruction. God's Spirit endows persons with the gifts required for their calling. This Exodus

passage describes in very specific terms the artistic abilities that
Bezalel used in crafting the tabernacle. In a similar fashion,
teaching can be viewed as a craft requiring specific skills and
artistic sensitivities. Teaching, like the construction and adorn-
ment of the tabernacle, can be anointed by the Holy Spirit to
accomplish God's purposes.

It must also be noted that some of the artistic gifts of the faith
community were used initially and idolatrously in the construction of the golden calf (Exod. 32). God's judgment confronted this misuse of gifts. All the gifts and abilities that individuals possess are from God and, if surrendered to God, can
become vehicles for spiritual ministry. In commenting on the
Spirit's empowerment for ministry, Erickson purports that when
"the temple was rebuilt by Zerubbabel after the Babylonian cap-
tivity, there was a similar endowment: 'Not by might nor by
power, but by my spirit, says the Lord of hosts'" (Zech. 4:6).[7]
The recognition of the Spirit's enablement for ministry from the
inception of life and the use of diverse skills and abilities apply
to teaching and the developed craft it requires for effective learning. Gifts can be used for the construction and perpetuation of
community life just as they were used to construct tabernacles
and temples for the nation of Israel.

One striking example of teaching ministry in the Old Testament is from the Book of Nehemiah. Chapter 8 records a corporate renewal as Ezra stands to read the law that had been long
forgotten in the life of the faith community. As priest and pas-
tor-teacher, Ezra preaches from a pulpit. He speaks from six
o'clock in the morning until noon. All those who could understand were assembled for this occasion. The distinctive teaching ministry in this setting is the work of the Levites, who fostered understanding by circulating through the crowd and
interpreting Ezra's words in smaller groups. The Levites are com-
parable to those called to be small group teachers in Christian
churches, interpreting Scripture and instructing the people in
God's ways. The writer of Ezekiel grasped the importance of the
Levites' ministry by observing that "they shall teach my people
the difference between the holy and the common, and show
them how to distinguish between the unclean and the clean. In
a controversy they shall act as judges, and they shall decide it

according to my judgments" (Ezek. 44:23–24). For teaching ministry as for leadership, a spirit of wisdom is essential as described in the example of Joshua (Deut. 34:9). The ability to sustain such a ministry requires a devotion to God that results from the outpouring of the Spirit (Isa. 44:3–5).[8]

The Old Testament bore witness to a coming time when the Spirit would have a fuller and more extensive ministry. This is made explicit in Joel 2:28–29: "Then afterward I will pour out my spirit on all flesh; your sons and your daughters shall prophesy, your old men shall dream dreams, and your young men shall see visions. Even on the male and female slaves, in those days, I will pour out my spirit."[9] Christians associate this prophecy with the coming of the Spirit at Pentecost in fulfillment of Jesus' promise. The coming of the Spirit upon the church enabled an extensive teaching ministry that Jesus described in Matthew 28:18–20:

> And Jesus came and said to them, "All authority in heaven and on earth has been given to me. Go therefore and make disciples of all nations, baptizing them in the name of the Father and of the Son and of the Holy Spirit, and teaching them to obey everything that I have commanded you. And remember, I am with you always, to the end of the age."

The Spirit in the Church's Teaching Ministry and Mission

Jesus assured his disciples of empowerment and enablement in his words at the ascension: "But you will receive power when the Holy Spirit has come upon you" (Acts 1:8). This echoes his message in John 16:13: "When the Spirit of truth comes, he will guide you into all truth." With the departure of the Master Teacher from earth, his disciples rely upon the Holy Spirit to guide and direct their ministries. The Holy Spirit is present at the birth of the Christian church at Pentecost (Acts 2:1–13) and is prominent in the accounts of the early church throughout the Book of Acts. The Holy Spirit was and is present to undergird the efforts of the church to teach and speak with authority. The Holy Spirit works to sustain, nurture, probe, and challenge the

Christian church in ways that accomplish Jesus Christ's agenda
for the world. The Holy Spirit testifies of Christ and inspired the
writers of Scripture. The Holy Spirit illumines the hearts and
minds of those who seek to understand, live by, and teach the
Scriptures. This follows the same pattern noted for Ezra in the
Old Testament (Ezra 7:10). This agenda takes shape in relation
to the values and perspectives of Christ's reign, the kingdom of
God, which is the content of his teaching. The authority of the
Spirit is actively expressed in accomplishing God's mission in
the world and in sustaining the active partnership of Christian
believers in that mission.[10]

The authority of the Holy Spirit in teaching can be explored
in relation to the authoritative Word of God and its role in teaching. God's Word is creative, living, and written. The creative
Word is described in both Genesis 1 and John 1, where God is
revealed in creation. As the Spirit sweeps over the face of the
waters, all things are created. As the Spirit moves over the assembled disciples of Jesus, the Christian church is created (Acts 2).
The creative Word is still active in the world, disclosing God and
creating new possibilities as persons respond to God's call to
teach and to wrestle with both special and general revelation.[11]
The Holy Spirit sustains Christians in their spiritual warfare as
they take up the sword of the Spirit, which is the Word of God
(Eph. 6:10–17).

Jesus Christ, the living Word, encounters persons through
the active presence and ministry of the Holy Spirit. The living
Word is a person, and his ministry relates to the individuals
engaged in teaching and learning, namely, those called as educators and students. The Holy Spirit is identified as the Spirit of
Christ who makes available to humankind the surpassing grace
of the crucified one in whom grace and truth have come (John
1:16).[12] Truth unfolds in the life of the faith community through
the ministries of proclamation, fellowship, service, advocacy,
and worship. Teaching provides the occasion to discern the connections across these ministries that serve to accomplish God's
mission in the world.[13]

The written Word is the essential source for authoritative
teaching. God's special revelation is through the person and
work of Jesus Christ as the living Word and through the Scrip-

tures as the written Word. The Holy Spirit inspired the initial writing and compilation of the Scriptures. The Holy Spirit also illuminates those who seek to teach the Scriptures or to be taught by them. The written Word provides the foundational, but not exhaustive, content for authoritative teaching in the Christian faith. A particular danger for some Christians is the view that the written Word is the believers' exhaustive authority. Such a view leads to biblicism, a view that the writers of Scripture did not take. With the written Word, Christians have an authoritative source that requires careful and discerning interpretation.[14] Such interpretation requires openness to the continuing ministry of the Holy Spirit as "ever new light and truth breaks forth from God's Holy Word."[15] As Paul suggested to Timothy, diligence is required in interpretation: "Do your best to present yourself to God as one approved by him, a worker who has no need to be ashamed, rightly explaining the word of truth" (2 Tim. 2:15).

With the coming of the Spirit at Pentecost, a new age of teaching began that continues to this day. The Apostle Paul, along with other New Testament writers, was instrumental in expounding the Spirit's educative role while being a model for teaching himself (1 Cor. 11:1). The Spirit's indwelling presence enabled believers to appropriate what God *in* us could mean for education in the ways of God. In the Book of Acts, believers were known as followers of "the Way" (Acts 9:2) made explicit in the life, death, and resurrection of Jesus. The Spirit's coming was part of Jesus' plan and enabled a ministry continuing beyond his earthly ministry of three years. The Spirit would also disclose truth that the disciples were unable to bear before Jesus' ascension (John 16:12–15). The process of discerning truth is a particular challenge with contending truth claims.[16]

"In Jesus' teaching we find an especially strong emphasis on the work of the Holy Spirit in initiating persons into the Christian life."[17] The educational commission given to Jesus' followers of making disciples and teaching them to obey everything that Jesus himself taught (Matt. 28:18–20) is a monumental task. The only possible way to fulfill this commission is to rely upon Jesus' promise in verse 20 to always be with us. Jesus' promise is fulfilled in the Spirit's indwelling and filling of believers. "Jesus taught that the Spirit's activity is essential in both conversion, which from the human perspective is the beginning of the Christian life, and regeneration, which from God's perspective is its beginning."[18] With a focus on individual persons, Erickson explains the Spirit's work in both conversion and regeneration as the goals of Christian teaching:

> Conversion is the human's turning to God. It consists of a negative and a positive element: repentance, that is, abandonment of sin; and faith, that is, acceptance of the promises and the work of Christ. Jesus spoke especially of repentance, and specifically of conviction of sin, which is the prerequisite of repentance. He said, "When he [the Counselor] comes, he will convict the world of guilt in regard to sin and righteousness and judgment: in regard to sin, because men do not believe in me; in regard to righteousness, because I am going to the Father, where you can see me no longer; and in regard to judgment, because the prince of this world now stands condemned" (John 16:8–11). Without this work of the Holy Spirit, there can be no conversion.
>
> Regeneration is the miraculous transformation of the individual and implantation of spiritual energy. Jesus made very clear to Nicodemus that regeneration is essential to acceptance by the Father: "I tell you the truth, no one can see the kingdom of God unless he is born again . . . no one can enter the kingdom of God unless he is born of water and the Spirit. Flesh gives birth to flesh, but Spirit gives birth to spirit" (John 3:3, 5–6). Clearly, regeneration is a supernatural occurrence, and the Holy Spirit is the agent who produces it. The flesh (i.e., human effort) is not capable of effecting this transformation. Nor can this transformation even be comprehended by the human intellect. Jesus in fact likened this work of the Spirit to the blowing of the wind: "The wind blows wherever it pleases. You hear its sound, but you cannot tell where it comes from or where it is going. So it is with everyone born of the Spirit" (v. 8).[19]

The teaching task of making disciples requires partnership with the Holy Spirit if conversion and regeneration are ever to be possible. Conversion is one of the primary purposes of Christian education.[20] Erickson's descriptions of conversion and regeneration do not emphasize the communal and corporate dimensions of the Christian life that are also works of the Spirit.

Through conversion and regeneration, persons are brought into relationship with the Trinity and the faith community. Personal and corporate communion with the Trinity require the consistent prayer life of the Christian teacher for the Holy Spirit to transform the lives of students.

Beyond initiation into the Christian life, the Holy Spirit's ministry is crucial for sustaining individuals in the Christian community who work to influence wider society as salt and light in the world. Teaching plays a major role in the ongoing ministries of sanctification, edification, and social witness and action. Sanctification is the process of transforming Christian persons increasingly to the image of Christ. Teaching enables Christians to grasp new dimensions of their discipleship, new areas to allow God's Spirit to work through them and despite them. Edification is the mutual building up of Christian persons as they seek the common good and minister corporately in the gathered church. Teaching provides occasions for Christians to reflect together on the meaning of their faith and its outworking in the world. Social witness and action provide the opportunity for ministry in relating Christian values to the issues and problems of wider society and the world. The church scattered in the world can make a difference. Teaching enables and equips Christians to make connections between their discipleship and citizenship in various public arenas. Such engagement with the world calls for the development of a public theology that struggles with how the lordship of Christ relates to all of creation.[21]

Christians anticipate the future reign of Christ, but they also work for the transformation of society at points where it undermines the fullness of humanity manifested in Jesus Christ. A less comprehensive educational agenda fails to address all of creation that God has sought to redeem in Jesus Christ and limits the transformative potential of the Holy Spirit. God's Spirit hovers or broods over all that was created in the Genesis account and over all humanity's engagement with the re-creation made possible in Jesus Christ. The visions of John 1, Colossians 1, Hebrews 1, and Revelation 1 provide a wide range for Christian teachers to consider in relating their faith to life in the world. In these key christological passages, Christ is affirmed as having significance for all of life. He is the *logos*, the Word

(John 1); the image of the invisible God revealed throughout creation (Col. 1); the reflection of God's glory (Heb. 1); and the first and last living one, the Alpha and the Omega (Rev. 1).[22] The work of the Spirit of Christ is enabling Christians to understand and live in the light of Christ's reign. The task before Christian teachers is to "take every thought captive to obey Christ" (2 Cor. 10:5) in teaching Jesus' disciples to obey everything he commanded (Matt. 28:20). This is a task requiring the work of God's Spirit to disclose truth and discern wisdom. It is a task calling for a radical transformation of persons by renewing their minds (Rom. 12:2). For such a teaching ministry, the Holy Spirit is indispensable.

The Holy Spirit is identified in the Scriptures as "the Spirit of truth" (John 15:26) who will guide Jesus' disciples into all truth (John 16:13). Those who teach and learn must be sensitive and open to the gentle promptings of the Spirit in their search for truth. The challenge in our pluralistic age is to teach both with a liberating spirit and in communion with the liberating Spirit of God. The challenge for Christians is to teach with authority as persons called and sent by God. This authority is authenticated through the lives and actions of teachers.[23] In this, the truth is incarnate.

The search for truth in biblical currency focuses on wisdom. Paul's teaching ministry as described in 1 Corinthians provides insights on wisdom from the Holy Spirit. According to biblical sources, wisdom is viewing life from God's perspective and responding with the grace, peace, understanding, and freedom God gives. Pope John Paul XXIII defined wisdom as "truth, that by God's grace, moves from the mind to the heart in order to move us to live and act on it."[24] In 1 Corinthians 2:6–16, Paul's focus is wisdom from God, the source of which is the Holy Spirit. Paul teaches in words taught by the Spirit, expressing spiritual truths in spiritual terms. The reception of these words also requires a work of the Spirit in the lives of his hearers or readers. A person without the Spirit does not accept the things that come from the Spirit. Paul reflects the words of Jesus to his disciples: "But the Advocate, the Holy Spirit, whom the Father will send in my name, will teach you everything, and remind you of all that I have said to you" (John 14:26). "When the Spirit of truth comes, he will guide you into all the truth; for he will not speak on his own, but will speak whatever he hears, and he will declare to you the things that are to come" (John 16:13). The Holy Spirit, whose responsibility is to teach believers all things and remind them of Jesus' teachings, equips the Christian educator to effectively minister and releases the creativity necessary to appropriately share and understand Christian truths.[25]

Effective teaching and learning require the continuing presence and work of the Holy Spirit today. Teaching is described as one of the gifts bestowed upon the church by Christ through the Holy Spirit (Rom. 12:3–8; 1 Cor. 12:27–31; Eph. 4:7–13; 1 Pet. 4:10–11). Teaching is not only a Spirit-endowed and Spirit-motivated gift; it also requires that the teacher be continually filled and guided by the Holy Spirit in the process of teaching (Eph. 4:29–32; 5:15–20). The spiritual dimensions of education are foundational from a New Testament perspective.[26] John Westerhoff affirms this in his work *Spiritual Life: The Foundation for Preaching and Teaching*.[27] Westerhoff defines the spiritual life that is the foundation of teaching as "ordinary, everyday life lived in an ever-deepening and loving relationship to God and therefore to one's true or healthy self, all people, and the whole of creation."[28] The guidelines for this loving relationship are captured in the two great commandments of loving God above all and loving our neighbor as ourselves.[29] Jesus provides a model for this love in his own teaching ministry and offers a new commandment, namely, that we love one another just as he has loved us (John 13:34–35; 15:12). The love required for the spiritual ministry of teaching has a divine source in the Holy Spirit: "God's love has been poured into our hearts through the Holy Spirit that has been given to us" (Rom. 5:5). What God and Jesus command of us in teaching is provided through the gift of the Holy Spirit. This makes sense in Paul's understanding of the work of God's Spirit. He poses a question that teachers can ask themselves: "He who did not withhold his own Son, but gave him up for all of us, will he not with him also give us everything else?" (Rom. 8:32). God knows we need love to care for others in our teaching and provides the blessed Holy Spirit as a source of Christ's love *in* us, *in* our hearts to share with others.

Christian Spirituality: A Relationship with the Holy Spirit

Interest in spirituality persists in the field of education, but clarity is required in understanding a Christian perspective on spirituality. Justo González notes that the basis for Christian spirituality is the Third Person of the Trinity. One is spiritual because of the presence and indwelling of the Holy Spirit. A spiritual person, a spiritual teacher, is one in whom the Spirit of the Lord dwells.[30]

> A spirituality without the Holy Spirit is a scandal in Christian faith and in Christian teaching. Christian spirituality is a way of deepening the experience of God's active presence through the work of the Holy Spirit in one's life, in the life of the church, and in the history of the world. Christian spirituality is about opening oneself to the healing power of the Spirit that enables persons to become whole and reconciled with God, with themselves, and with the world. The world is God's creation and the object of God's love (John 3:16). The world is in need of teachers who give evidence of that love by manifesting the distinct marks of Christian spirituality.[31]

How is such spirituality nurtured? An ecumenical study in 1987 proposed ten characteristics of Christian spirituality to guide educators in the spiritual development of students:

1. Reconciling and integrative,
2. Incarnational,
3. Rooted in Scripture and nourished in prayer,
4. Costly and self-giving,
5. Life-giving and liberative,
6. Rooted in community and centered in worship,
7. Expressed in service and witness,
8. Waiting for God's surprises,
9. Unfolding the loving purposes of God on earth, and

10. Open to the wider Christian church and truths shared by other religious faiths.[32]

These qualities continue to be insightful in fostering a relationship with the Holy Spirit in teaching.

James Loder captures the dynamics and logic of our relationship with the Holy Spirit by considering the Reformed understanding of the *Spiritus Creator*. This understanding embraces the transformational potential of the relationship between individuals and the Spirit. Loder notes, "Although distinctly different in origin, destiny, and magnitude, the human spirit and Divine Spirit are made for each other, according to a relationality ultimately designed to replicate the relationality of the divine and the human in the person of Jesus Christ."[33] The Holy Spirit brings to fruition the blessings of the new creation in Jesus Christ. The Holy Spirit superintends the transformation processes of conversion, sanctification, edification, and mission (see chapter 2). In addition to these general dimensions, the Spirit confronts, corrects, directs, and resurrects when our teaching efforts fail to fulfill God's purposes and promise of new life. God's Spirit graciously works when, despite our best efforts, no transformation is evident or seems possible. Teachers can celebrate the transformative learning made possible by the Spirit while prayerfully awaiting the future transformation God requires.

Millard Erickson provides further insight for Spirit-filled teaching by outlining six implications of the work of the Spirit:

1. The gifts that we have are bestowals upon us by the Holy Spirit. We should recognize that they are not our own accomplishments. They are intended to be used in the fulfillment of his plan.

2. The Holy Spirit empowers believers in their Christian lives and service. Personal inadequacies should not deter or discourage us.

3. The Holy Spirit dispenses his gifts to the church wisely and sovereignly. Possession or lack of a particular gift is

no cause for pride or regret. His gifts are not rewards to those who seek or qualify for them.

4. No one gift is for everyone, and no one person has every gift. The fellowship of the body is needed for full spiritual development of the individual believer.

5. We may rely on the Holy Spirit to give us understanding of the Word of God and to guide us into his will for us.

6. It is appropriate to direct prayer to the Holy Spirit, just as to the Father and the Son, as well as to the Triune God. In such prayers we will thank him for and especially ask him to continue, the unique work that he does in us.[34]

Erickson's insights help us better understand the work of the Holy Spirit in teaching. First, the gift of teaching is one that the Spirit bestows. However, this gift is given for the common good and to accomplish God's purposes in the world. Second, the Holy Spirit empowers certain Christians to teach. Those with the teaching gift are enabled to exercise it even in the face of conflict or opposition such as Jesus encountered in his hometown of Nazareth. Third, the Spirit gives teaching gifts in a discerning fashion to accomplish God's purposes for the Christian church. Teaching gifts are not given for self-aggrandizement but for service. Fourth, exercising diverse teaching gifts in a mutual and supportive way is crucial for the edification of the entire church as well as individual persons. Fifth, the Holy Spirit plays a crucial role in illuminating the Word of God, which is a central task in Christian teaching. Sixth, prayer for the Spirit's work should undergird all efforts of Christian teaching and learning. Erickson's implications also provide general guidelines for the exercise of spiritual teaching. A teacher needs to have connections that are more explicit. What connections can be proposed between the Holy Spirit and teaching? How does the Holy Spirit undergird each of the three phases of teaching that I have proposed—preparation, instruction, and evaluation? Julie Gorman refers to these three phases as the "triple crown" of teaching.[35] Here I explore them in relation to a spirituality of teaching.

A Spirituality of Teaching

Parker Palmer brought attention to the spirituality of education in his work *To Know As We Are Known: A Spirituality of Education*.[36] He introduced the importance of assessing the connection between teaching and our underlying interests, passions, or loves. Palmer names three distinct human interests that can be associated with different teaching conceptions and practices: control, curiosity, and compassion. Each of these interests fosters a distinct corporate spirituality that remains implicit in the vast majority of teaching settings. A fourth interest that we might add to Palmer's trinity is conflict as it relates to control. The student seeks, through applied empirical and analytical study, to gain control over a body of knowledge. This is the dominant cultural preoccupation or passion in a technological society such as the United States. The knowledge gained through speculative, historical, and hermeneutical study seeks to discover knowledge as an end in itself, to satisfy curiosity. This is the dominant cultural passion that emerged from the Greek educational heritage and is affirmed in more traditional, classical, and liberal arts teaching traditions. The knowledge that liberates is one that Palmer finds described in 1 Corinthians 8:1–3: "Now concerning food sacrificed to idols: we know that 'all of us possess knowledge.' Knowledge puffs up, but love builds up. Anyone who claims to know something does not yet have the necessary knowledge; but anyone who loves God is known by [God]." This knowledge is associated with compassion or love.[37] The additional interest of conflict is suggested by 2 Corinthians 10:4–5: "We destroy arguments and every proud obstacle raised up against the knowledge of God, and we take every thought captive to obey Christ." Conflict indicates the spiritual battle that is waged within persons, communities, and the world in Christian teaching.

Palmer's identification of compassion or love as the highest interest to guide teaching resonates with the two great commandments spoken by Jesus. To love God with all of our hearts, souls, minds, and strength is the first commandment for life and therefore for education. However, the second commandment is intimately connected in loving our neighbors as ourselves. Love for God whom we cannot see finds direct expression in how we relate to those persons we see and interact with each day. Jesus made this explicit connection in Matthew 25:31–46 in describing the judgment of the nations. Our response to the hungry, thirsty, strangers, naked, sick, and imprisoned is equated with our response to Jesus himself. If we cannot love those we see, how can we expect to know and love God revealed in the face of Jesus Christ? Does our knowledge of God issue in acts of love for the marginalized? Augustine proposed a definition for spirituality that helps to clarify these issues. He defined spirituality as the *ordo armoris* or order of our loves:

> Our spirituality is not what we explicitly express, nor what we profess to believe, but how we order our loves. That ordering may be unarticulated, even quite unconscious, but the resultant spirituality pervades our whole life and involves our whole person. Our stewardship of time, energy, and substance reflects the way we live out and express the ordering of our loves. . . . There can be and indeed is what can be called a spirituality of consumerism, a spirituality of security, a spirituality of the avoidance of pain, or even a spirituality of destructive violence.[38]

Christians daily contend with a host of spiritualities that conflict with God's purposes for creation. Spiritual conflict on this level calls for making choices similar to those posed for Jesus' initial followers.

The connection between a Christian spirituality of love and teaching can be elaborated in terms of the requests Jesus made of his disciples. His requests suggest an order of loves and pose conflict with the world's standard spiritualities. The order of loves implicit in our lives is a vehicle for teaching. We know Jesus' disciples requested that he teach them to pray (Luke 11:1). This explicit request contains unspoken implications: teach us to worship in spirit and truth; teach us to study the Scriptures; teach us to serve others whatever their standing or situation; teach us to embrace the joy you model in all situations; teach us to confront evil and hypocrisy; and teach us to know God's presence in all of life. The exercise of love can often bring conflict as we confront those thoughts, actions, patterns, and structures that are not captive to Christ. These requests connect teaching and spiritual life as modeled in Jesus' ministry and that of his disciples. Costs are involved in following Jesus (Luke 9:21–27, 57–62).

Beyond those already noted, what specifically could be proposed to relate the person and work of the Holy Spirit to the three educational phases of preparation, instruction, and evaluation?

Preparation

In my work *Basics of Teaching for Christians*, I note that the preparation of a teacher's spirit or soul is one essential element for teaching. I also elaborate on how preparation also needs to include the teacher's heart, mind, and body.[39] This is a costly and comprehensive challenge. My earlier analysis should not suggest that the Holy Spirit only relates to the spirits of educators to the exclusion of their hearts, minds, and bodies. The immediate connection between individuals and the person of the Spirit may be through their spirits, but clearly the influences extend into all dimensions of a teacher's life. Also, the preparation phase and the Spirit's influence cannot be limited to teachers. The lives of students must be identified as a crucial dimension of the Spirit's ministry if any learning is to happen. In addition, the Spirit's work is honored in the context and content of teaching. How is this possible?

In relation to the teacher, the Holy Spirit's partnership begins with the person's birth and development. Because of sin we persistently resist this relationship. As grace abounds over a life fraught with spiritual struggles, the teacher's unique gifts, abilities, sensitivities, and skills are woven together by the Spirit's transforming presence. The Spirit works in calling the teacher to his or her particular ministry and desires openness to a daily filling to direct and empower the preparation for teaching. Prayer is essential in preparing as the teacher requests the Spirit's enlightenment and trusts in what he or she senses to be necessary in the particular teaching session. My own practice is to ask for the Spirit's guidance in relation to the particular audience and individuals I am being called to teach. Of course, this does not assure that everything I decide to teach will be in tune with what God's Spirit would have me teach. Nevertheless, the Spirit works *despite* my individual quirks, inadequacies, and sins. Though a definite gap exists between my will and God's will, I strive to discern the Spirit's leading in the various choices I make when preparing to teach. I am often humbled to see the fruits of efforts that I have fumbled through. I attribute the results to gaps in my preparation where the Holy Spirit graciously fills my deficits. My preparation may also include a conscious effort to appropriate the content in new ways. If the teaching material does not elicit passion and enthusiasm in me, it is not likely to connect with students. As Augustine noted, "One loving spirit sets another spirit on fire."[40] This requires prayer to increase love for students, for the content being taught, and for transformation of lives and hearts to become vessels of God's love and work in the world.

Preparation of participants relates to the issue of readiness. Adequately assessing the readiness of students in Christian teaching is complex and can be overwhelming considering the variety of variables that influence persons individually, corporately, and contextually. Yet, there is a resource person who is available—the Holy Spirit. The Spirit assists teachers in assessing student readiness and planning with prayer and reflection before the actual instruction. In considering the context for teaching, D. Campbell Wyckoff points to the divine as complementing both the natural and human aspects. The Holy Spirit is the determinative environmental presence. The challenge for teachers is to create those conditions where the Spirit of God can work most fruitfully in the lives of persons.[41]

Instruction

I sense the Spirit's work in instruction through the questions, responses, and actions of participants. Issues and problems not identified in my preparation provide occasions to be open to the Spirit's leading. They can also serve as distractions. Therefore, discernment is required. Part of the teaching task is to creatively weave together student responses with the immediate content and with the wider context of teaching. Being aware of what students bring with them into the classroom setting can signal this. My practice is to arrive at least fifteen minutes before the appointed class time in order to interact with students and discern their presenting agendas. Observation and interaction just before instruction can provide helpful clues for possible points of connection between the content and the participants. Dealing with unexpected responses also provides an opportunity to silently pray for the Spirit's guidance or to seek the discernment of the entire group. Experience and discernment are helpful companions for educators at this point. They provide material for evaluation as the teacher solicits the wisdom of colleagues after the actual teaching event.

Instruction is a risky venture with a host of variables that affect the actual experience for both students and teachers. From the perspective of Christianity, reliance on the presence of the Holy Spirit provides both an anchor for stability and a strong wind to launch out in creative ways. This presents a paradox for teachers. Risks can be taken in new instructional ventures knowing that their basic security is not threatened. While this may place teachers in difficult situations, partnership with the Holy Spirit enables them to have courage. Paul's words to Timothy can reassure educators: "For God did not give us a spirit of cowardice, but rather a spirit of power and of love and of self-discipline" (2 Tim. 1:7).

Parker Palmer explores this dimension of teaching in his work *The Courage to Teach*.[42] Teachers proclaim who they are in the instructional act. Because of a relationship with the Holy Spirit, Christian teachers are able to proclaim that they are children of God with all of their weaknesses and strengths. The Holy Spirit is the Spirit of adoption described by Paul in Romans 8:14–17:

> For all who are led by the Spirit of God are children of God. For you did not receive a spirit of slavery to fall back into fear, but you have received a spirit of adoption. When we cry, "Abba! Father!" it is that very Spirit bearing witness with our spirit that we are children of God, and if children, then heirs, heirs of God

and joint heirs with Christ—if, in fact, we suffer with him so that
we may also be glorified with him.

In the teaching ministry, we face the risks, acknowledging our
primary relationship as children of God and coheirs with Jesus
Christ.

Courage is a gift bestowed by the Spirit on teachers and all
who serve in ministry. It is required to address conflict and to
confront various issues, including spiritual ones. Courage
granted by the Spirit provides hope for Christian teachers. In
the words of one great Christian teacher, "Hope has two lovely
daughters, anger and courage. Anger at the way things are, and
courage to see that they need not remain as they are."[43] Christian educators are called to have courage in addressing situations both inside and outside the classroom. Instructing with
hope and courage assumes that we have clarity regarding the
authority of our teaching ministry. Norman DeJong identifies
authority as the first rung on a ladder for developing an educational philosophy. Authority is followed by a view of persons,
purposes and goals, structural organization, implementation,
and evaluation.[44] Teaching with authority and courage is a
dimension of ministering to others with the hope that transformation can occur. God's Spirit *in* us assures Christian teachers
of hope and empowerment in their calling and provides perspective for meeting the daily challenges of teaching.

In ministry, teachers are conscious of how persons are at various stages of development. These levels provide a divine blueprint for human growth. Nevertheless, while accommodating
developmental descriptions, Christian teachers need not follow
them in such predetermined ways, recognizing the priority of
divine over human elements. God's Spirit can intrude on the
developmental process in unanticipated ways to bring about
transformation in the lives of individuals and groups. The Holy
Spirit encounters human spirits in gracious ways that may not
always be predicted by developmental ages and stages. "Development is not destiny."[45] In my experience, a child's comments
can often provide insight and perspective that surrounding
adults have failed to see. This allows for serendipity and surprise
in the instructional process. The sovereign operation of the Holy

Spirit is honored. The work of the Spirit may build upon and/or negate existing elements of development to bring a creative and dynamic integration that was not otherwise possible. James Loder and Jim Neidhardt describe this possibility as a "knight's move," the creative act of Christ's Spirit to bring transformation in unpredictable and discontinuous ways within the human game of life.[46] Actually discerning the Spirit's work may only be possible with evaluation.

Evaluation

Christians recognize that the Holy Spirit applies, complements, and corrects human teaching. Evaluation provides an opportunity to gain perspective on these processes of sanctification and edification. The larger human quest for truth in education must be seen in relation to God being the source of all truth. While the Holy Spirit enlightens minds to discern truth through special and general revelation as shared in the instructional process, communal evaluation serves to confirm or refute that truth. The Spirit also enables persons to live in accordance with the truths disclosed or discovered in instruction. Evaluation provides the opportunity to assess the fruits of teaching in the lives of students. The Holy Spirit is the agent working for long-term personal and social transformation among persons in the world. Christian educators must, therefore, evaluate the workings of the Spirit in the areas of renewal and transformation.

Ways of cooperating with the Holy Spirit both inside and outside of the classroom can be evaluated. Recognizing transformation and renewal becomes a basis for thanksgiving and celebration in evaluation.[47] In addition, the Holy Spirit's work as advocate may suggest areas for further ministry as teachers follow up their instruction in subsequent sessions or contacts outside the classroom setting. Christian educators are to be advocates for those persons and concerns that are close to the heart of God. In commenting on the place of advocacy in ministry, Arthur Becker identifies three aspects: the correction of past injustice, the positive present pursuit of justice, and the prevention of future injustice.[48] In evaluation, teachers consider whether they have been faithful to advocacy that is upon the heart of the Holy Spirit. How does this happen?

In the work *Basics of Teaching for Christians*, I propose five values that correspond to the five tasks of the Christian church that will be discussed in chapter 6.[49] The five tasks are five gifts the Holy Spirit has given to the church for teaching: proclamation, community formation, service, advocacy, and worship. The five corresponding values for teaching are truth, love, faith, hope, and joy. Related to each of these is a call for teachers in evaluating their teaching. I propose the following pairings of Christian values that provide a basis for evaluation: *truth*—a call for integrity; *love*—a call for care; *faith*—a call for action; *hope*—a call for courage; and *joy*—a call for celebration. In evaluation, teachers seek the discernment of the Spirit to assess the fruits of their efforts. Specifically, teachers can ask the following: How has the teaching manifested an integrity that glorifies God? How has care been exercised for the content, persons, and context of this teaching? How have the teachers' actions and learning activities fulfilled the instructional goals and objectives? How has the teaching fostered a sense of hope for the lives and ministries of participants? How has a sense of joy permeated the teaching? While more specific questions are possible, these serve to illustrate broad areas for evaluation. Christian educators can directly inquire how the Spirit has worked in the preparation, instruction, and evaluation phases of teaching. This assumes that some time has been devoted to formal or informal evaluation during and after the instruction.

In her classic work *Education That Is Christian*, Lois LeBar outlines several guidelines for the work of the Spirit in teaching that provide additional areas for potential evaluation:

THE HOLY SPIRIT IN THE TEACHER

1. The Holy Spirit seeks to become our life, deeper than thought or feeling.
2. The Spirit works through the written Word to exalt the living Christ of the cross.
3. The only work that counts is the Spirit's work through us.

4. Our part is to receive the divine guidance and power that the Spirit comes to give.

5. We must practice active submission to the Holy Spirit and be passive toward the strivings of the self-life.

THE HOLY SPIRIT IN THE PROCESS OF TEACHING

1. We must keep the person of Christ central rather than the work [of teaching].

2. Insight that is both spiritual and educational enables the leader to penetrate deeply into personality.

3. It is the peculiar ministry of the Holy Spirit to make the outer Word an inner experience.

4. All problems are rooted in the spiritual, yet they also need solutions on the human level.

5. Although we make thorough preparation in the Spirit ahead of time, we should be ready for the Spirit's leading during the lesson.[50]

Each of LeBar's guidelines for both the teacher and the teaching process suggests dimensions of a spiritual assessment that honors the Holy Spirit. They provide perspective on the warning from James 3:1–2: "Not many of you should become teachers, my brothers and sisters, for you know that we who teach will be judged with greater strictness. For all of us make many mistakes." God's grace, present in the person and work of the Spirit, is available to teachers as we honestly evaluate our teaching efforts. The dynamics of the Spirit's work vary with individuals and their distinctive history, character, age, gender, life experience, developmental stage, and cultural and community connections. Mystery attends the Spirit's ministry. This chapter only hints at the spiritual depths of teaching God intends.

Conclusion

This fourth chapter has explored God's continuing work *in* us through the person of the Holy Spirit. The blessed Comforter gifted to the church at Pentecost undergirds the teaching ministry. The Spirit comes alongside those of us who teach to form a divine-human partnership fraught with wonder and dread. This is both a marvel and a mystery that sustains teachers in their diverse ministries. Peter Hodgson describes the teaching work of God's Spirit this way:

> God "teaches" through the "educing," or leading forth, of the human spirit into the widest range of its potentialities. Through the interaction of Spirit and spirit, the possible becomes actual, the ideal becomes real, truth becomes known, beauty takes shape, the good enters into practice. This is the work of God's Spirit.
>
> "Wisdom" *(sophia)* defines the kind of Spirit that God's Spirit is—not a possessing, displacing, controlling, or abandoning Spirit, but a persuading, educing, nurturing, communicating, teaching Spirit, acting in profound interaction with human spirit, indeed the whole cosmos. Education as growth in wisdom is evoked by God's Wisdom *(sophia tou theou)* which challenges the foolishness of worldly wisdom *(sophia tou kosmou)* (1 Cor. 1:18–2:13).[51]

Hodgson's description affirms the essential teaching of this chapter: God *in* us through the person and work of the Holy Spirit assures us of an empowered partnership for teaching. The nature of this partnership is further explored in chapter 5 which discusses the ministry and mission of the Christian church, God *through* us.

FIVE

GOD THROUGH US: THE CHURCH AND TEACHING

The Christian church stands in relationship with God because of the ministries of God the Father, Son, and Spirit.[1] The life of the Trinity *(perichoresis)* portrays what the church is intended to be. The church has multiple roles as clergy and laity with a variety of gifts (differentiation and diversity). It celebrates an eternal bond maintained by the Holy Spirit (unity) and has a cooperative and collaborative mission in the world guided by Jesus' commandments (an order of loves). Christians have their primary identity in communion with the Triune God on both the personal and corporate levels of life. Christians are formed into a communal life that enables them to realize their individual callings (vocation) and their corporate calling as God's people in the world. The Apostle Paul identifies this reality in 1 Corinthians 12:4–7: "Now there are varieties of gifts, but the same Spirit; and there are varieties of services, but the same Lord; and there are varieties of activities, but it is the same God who activates all of them in everyone. To each is given the manifestation of the Spirit for the common good." The varieties of gifts, services, and activities that form a vocation engage Christians in their relationships with the Holy Spirit, Jesus Christ, and God the Father as noted in this passage. That these blessings and endowments of God's grace are explicitly given for "the common good" is too often lost in our age of conspicuous consumption that stresses individualism at the expense of community.

The restoration and renewal of the common good require that Christians affirm their primary identities. Such a renewal will foster the teaching ministries of the Christian church and provide one basis for making educational connections between ecclesiology (the study of the church) and missiology (the study of Christian mission). Millard Erickson suggests that an implicit trinitarianism is found in the primary images that Paul used to describe the New Testament church as the people of God, the body of Christ, and the temple of the Holy Spirit.[2] These three images provide insights for the teaching ministry of the church. On a personal level that complements our corporate ecclesial identity, each Christian can be identified as a child of God, a disciple and friend of Jesus Christ, and a vessel of the Holy Spirit. Both corporate and personal identities apply to the teaching ministry. In addition to the trinitarian identity of the Christian church, an understanding of the marks of the church as one, holy, catholic, and apostolic enhances the corporate sense of ministry in a time when a party or tribal spirit too often dominates relationships among Christians.

God works *through* the church to accomplish the divine purposes and specific tasks it has been assigned. I have identified those tasks as proclamation *(kerygma)*, community formation *(koinonia)*, service *(diakonia)*, advocacy *(propheteia)*, and worship *(leitourgia)*.[3] Note that the teaching task or *didache* is not named as one of the five tasks. Why is this the case? I believe that teaching serves as the connective membrane linking these five tasks to form a vital and living body of ministry and mission in the world. This is suggested in 1 Corinthians 12:4–7 as quoted above. Teaching first serves to sustain the body of Christ in its varieties of service. Teaching also serves to form the corporate identity as God's people discern their common good in fulfilling the Father's purposes in the world. Likewise, teaching serves to sustain the varieties of gifts as the structure that supports and moves with the Holy Spirit on the tabernacle journey that began at Pentecost and continues until the final consummation. The Trinity works and manifests God *through* us in an amazing variety of teaching ministries and missions that result in praise and glory to our eternal teacher.

The five tasks I list have direct parallels with the five church models that Avery Dulles has identified in his work *Models of the Church*. The models are institution *(propheteia)*, mystical communion *(koinonia)*, sacrament *(leitourgia)*, herald *(kerygma)*, and servant *(diakonia)*.[4] Churches tend to direct their lives in terms of one or more of these models. Dulles's models parallel the tasks of advocacy, fellowship or community formation, worship, proclamation, and service. These five tasks capture the priorities of God's activity in the world as made explicit in the earthly ministry of Jesus Christ and the continuing ministry of the Holy Spirit. Each task has expressions related to the inreach or ministry of gathered churches and to the outreach or mission of the church throughout the world. The tasks or models also serve to identify the gifts the Holy Spirit has sovereignly granted to the church for the common good (1 Cor. 12:7). With the faithful exercise of these spiritual gifts, each task serves as a mark of the church in the world and a dimension of its wider mission. Teaching serves as the means to prepare God's people for their gathered ministry times and their scattered mission.

A more detailed description of the five tasks of the church as they relate to teaching is provided in chapter 6. Nevertheless, it is important to note some particulars for our present discussion of the church. Proclamation *(kerygma)* suggests that Christian teachers present the essentials of the Christian story and foster the connection between both personal and communal story. Proclamation includes the invitation to embrace the Christian faith and follow Jesus Christ as Lord and Savior. Community formation or fellowship *(koinonia)* suggests that Christian teachers foster hospitality and caring relationships, including individual relationships with the Triune God. Such formation requires the gracious working of the Holy Spirit and the willingness of teachers to share themselves as well as their doctrine (1 Thess. 2:8; 1 Tim. 4:16). Service *(diakonia)* invites Christian teachers to model good works (1 Cor. 11:1) and to mentor others in the faith (Eph. 2:8–10). Speaking the truth in love (Eph. 4:15) includes loving actions that equip and encourage others to do the same through the diverse ministries and missions of the church. Advocacy *(propheteia)* requires courage to denounce actions, practices, policies, and structures that conflict with gospel understandings of the full life God intends for all persons and creation. Advocacy is a risk that stands in the prophetic tradition and with those who are marginalized and have no voice or will to embrace God's justice, peace, and hope. Worship *(leitourgia)* invites Christian teachers to praise, glorify, and celebrate the wonder and mystery of God in all of life. Worship is encouraged in the activities of study, creativity, and leisure that foster a sense of awe and reverence before God and the wondrous creation. This fivefold teaching ministry requires the dedicated efforts of laity and clergy who teach in a variety of settings.

The historical difference between laity and clergy has caused much division and conflict in the church. Difference and diversity should not cause division if they are not viewed as deficiency. As revealed in the life of the Trinity *(perichoresis)*, diversity and differentiation is balanced with unity, complementarity, and interdependence. This is also suggested by the Galilean principle in Jesus' life and ministry. Gabriel Fackre helpfully distinguishes the roles of clergy and laity in their complementary ministries and missions. He suggests that clergy have ministries of identity, whereas laity have ministries of vitality. By this he does not mean that clergy cannot be vital in faith or that laity cannot be identified with the faith, but that a functional division, a division in office, exists. Such a functional division serves to identify priorities in ministry and mission. Fackre also indicates the wider context of ministry and mission that emphasizes mutuality, partnership, and interdependence between laity and clergy in their diverse tasks.[5] In fact, clergy are included in an understanding of laity as the people of God, the body of Christ, and the temple of the Holy Spirit. The ministries of identity and vitality are interdependent and call for a process of mutual edification in the life of the Christian church.

The varieties of teaching ministries and missions of the laity and clergy honor the place of diversity. As noted, the theme of diversity needs to be complemented by an affirmation of the unity that is present in the Trinity and sought after in the Christian church. Therefore, mutual edification also serves to maintain the unity of the church which the Apostle Paul speaks of in Ephesians 4:1–16.

Paul describes a unity of the church and a diversity of gifts that serve the ministry and mission of Christians. In my approach to Christian education, teaching serves as the ligaments of the body of Christ, joining and knitting together the diversity of gifts and equipping Christians for their diverse ministries.[6] Speaking the truth in love includes not only words but also actions that serve as an evangelical witness or testimony. Actions of service, advocacy, worship, community formation, and proclamation are an encouragement for the growth of Christ's body.

As the church responds to God's grace and love, Christians themselves gain a sense of clarity in their identities, missions, and mutual interdependence. As people of God, members of Christ's body, and vessels adorning the temple of the Holy Spirit, they affect the wider world in mission. Engaging the wider world is an expression of God's love (John 3:16) in accomplishing the divine purposes for all of creation. Here again the Trinity is a picture of what the church is intended to be in its mission. Teaching for this wider mission is a particular challenge for the third millennium. To engage the world in mission, the church must fulfill God's purposes in extending Christ's reign *through* the church. As followers of Jesus, Christians are assured of the continuing ministry of the Holy Spirit to fulfill their callings. They are also assured of a partnership with other believers in the past, present, and future. A vast company of witnesses is described by the writer of Hebrews to provide perspective and encouragement:

> Therefore, since we are surrounded by so great a cloud of witnesses, let us also lay aside every weight and the sin that clings so closely, and let us run with perseverance the race that is set before us, looking to Jesus the pioneer and perfecter of our faith, who for the sake of the joy that was set before him endured the cross, disregarding its shame, and has taken his seat at the right hand of the throne of God. (Heb. 12:1–2)

Jesus serves as the "pioneer and perfecter" and as the exemplar and model for the life that Christians are called to embrace (see chapter 3). The Holy Spirit indwells Christians, empowering and enabling them to follow Jesus in their ministries and missions (see chapter 4). Above all, God the Father reigns and God's sovereignty assures the church of ultimate security and fulfillment in this life and in the life to come (see chapter 6).

Teaching as the People of God

The church is called to be a distinct and separate people whose primary purpose is to glorify and enjoy God. This requires a primary allegiance and commitment to the creator as creatures receiving God's providential care, protection, and guidance. Christians' dependence on God as creator implies a stance of interdependence with all of creation and not just with humanity. For Christian teaching, this suggests both an appreciation of the wider educational ecology and one goal that fosters a sense of accountability to creation. As recipients of God's care, Christian teachers are to care for their students and for the wider cultural, social, political, economic, religious, intellectual, and ideological structures in which education occurs. Educational ecologies vary over time, and attention is required to assess the impact of larger systems upon any given educational encounter. The ultimate encounter in Christian teaching is between God and creatures. God as teacher uses a host of means to instruct persons, including both general and special revelation. God intends to fashion a people who are formed after the divine heart and mind. In our sin we resist this inheritance, but God offers a striking alternative. God is most wonderfully revealed in the person of Jesus Christ. God's written Word, the Bible, is the primary source for understanding Jesus and God's intentions for all creation.

Millard Erickson points out that "the concept of the church as the people of God emphasizes God's initiative in choosing them."[7] As chosen people, Christian educators need to discern how best to pursue God's activities in their particular ministries (1 Cor. 12:6). God's choosing has several implications. First, the wonder of God's choosing is noted by Paul in 1 Corinthians 1:27–31:

> But God chose what is foolish in the world to shame the wise;
> God chose what is weak in the world to shame the strong; God
> chose what is low and despised in the world, things that are not,
> to reduce to nothing things that are, so that no one might boast
> in the presence of God. He is the source of your life in Christ
> Jesus, who became for us wisdom from God, and righteousness
> and sanctification and redemption, in order that, as it is written,
> "Let the one who boasts, boast in the Lord."

Conflict arises between human predisposition and divine choice, for God chooses the *anawim* who are poor, humble, and weak before God and others.[8] Second, clarifying the nature and context of God's activities through the investment of time, energy, and talent is a matter of stewardship for those who are chosen. This is a lifelong challenge. As a child of God and an active participant with God's people in the world, the Christian teacher is accountable before God. This accountability to follow God's demands and meet God's expectations is complemented by the blessings and privileges of being adopted into God's family. Being able to address God as "Abba" implies a relationship that meets the deepest longings of the human heart for love, acceptance, and purpose. Life has meaning in light of communion with God and fulfilling God's will in our personal and corporate lives. The teaching ministry can help persons explore their deep questions about life such as, Where did I come from? Who am I? and Where am I going? Christianity provides a framework in which to explore meaning in relation to God's purposes and calling. Trinitarian grammar provides a framework in which to view all of life.

Erickson suggests that the church as the people of God has several implications. "God takes pride in them. He cares and protects his people; he keeps them 'as the apple of his eye' (Deut. 32:10). Finally, he expects that they will be his people without reservation and without dividing loyalty."[9] This care, protection, and pride applies to teaching ministries and invites committed Christian educators to do all for the glory of God (1 Cor. 6:20; 10:31; Eph. 3:20–21). This sets a high standard that calls for dedication and diligence and poses a daily spiritual challenge. The Old Testament model for dedication is Ezra: "For Ezra had set his heart to study the law of the LORD, and to do it, and to teach the statutes and ordinances in Israel" (Ezra 7:10). God's New Israel, the church, is called to a similar dedication or devotion. Whereas the sign of the old covenant was external circumcision of the flesh, "we find in the new covenant an inward circumcision of the heart."[10] Paul makes this clear in Romans 2:29: "Rather, a person is a Jew who is one inwardly, and real circumcision is a matter of the heart—it is spiritual and not literal. Such a person receives praise not from others but from God." For the Christian teacher, circumcision of the heart requires clarity of commitment and a dedication sustained through all of life's transitions and struggles. The costs of such dedication are real. They can be measured in terms of a host of options available to persons in developed nations and in terms of survival for the vast majority of the world's population. Regardless of position or circumstance, heart commitments must find expression in our use of finite time and energy as the people of God called to teach.

Teaching as the Body of Christ

As the body of Christ, the church is to follow the example of the Master Teacher. But more than an example, Jesus Christ serves as the coordinating and controlling head of the body with individual teachers linked to his loving leadership. This requires teachers to intentionally abide in Christ as disciples or followers who depend on him for our daily sustenance. Erickson notes that the image of the body of Christ "emphasizes that the church is the locus of Christ's activity just as his physical body during his earthly ministry."[11] The ministries of Christian teachers in public, private, religious, communal, and familial settings provide loci for Christ's activities in the world. Through its own teaching, the local church can clarify the connections for Christians across those diverse settings. It can communicate a sense of care through prayer and opportunities for recognition, dialogue, and equipping of persons for teaching service. Erickson further notes that "the image of the body of Christ also emphasizes the connection of the church, as a group of believers, with

Christ."[12] Here the church can foster the relationships teachers have with Christ and each other through its spiritual nurture and opportunities to grow in their personal and communal discipleship. Erickson indicates that "the image of the body of Christ also speaks of the interconnectedness between all the persons who make up the church."[13] Educators are in partnership with other Christians who exercise diverse gifts that need to be received and appreciated in mutual ministries. Erickson cites the mutuality within the body of Christ where "each believer encourages and builds up the others."[14] I have witnessed this when teachers have opportunities to share aspects of their ministries including discipline problems, creative possibilities, and practical skills that result in effective learning. Teachers' perspectives radically shift when they realize others have faced similar challenges and resolved issues they thought only they confronted. Opportunities for sharing foster the fellowship and sense of unity and universality that Erickson indicates is associated with the image of the body of Christ.[15]

The body of Christ teaches through its individual and corporate ministries. These include formal, nonformal, and informal encounters that provide "teachable moments." The most public opportunity for teaching is the worship service, which honors the reality of the living Christ through formal or informal observance of the liturgical year. Where two or three are gathered in Jesus' name (Matt. 18:20), there is an occasion for teaching. Jesus promises to be present among those who gather in his name. In such encounters, Christian educators are invited to discern the face and presence of Jesus in other persons as suggested in Matthew 25:31–46.

Teaching as the Temple of the Holy Spirit

The Gospel of Luke records the occasion of Jesus teaching in the temple at the age of twelve (Luke 2:41–51). The pattern of Jesus' teaching at this early age is repeated in his postresurrection encounter with two disciples on the Emmaus road (Luke 24:13–35). It is a threefold pattern of listening to what others are saying, questioning of teachers and disciples, and opening of the Scriptures to discern meaning or share understanding. In both cases, the teaching encounter results in amazement, wonder, and joy.

The same experience is possible for those who receive the promised power of the Holy Spirit to witness to the living Christ in their teaching ministries to the ends of the earth (Acts 1:8). The Spirit's person and ministry make this possible as Christians are formed and transformed into vessels for service. Just as Bezalel was filled with the Spirit in adorning the tabernacle (Exod. 31:2–5), so the Spirit-filled ministries of Christian teachers adorn God's dwelling as a tabernacle with his people in the church. Bezalel was assisted in his ministry by Oholiab, who was an "engraver, designer, and embroiderer in blue, purple, and crimson yarns, and in fine linen" (Exod. 38:23). Both Bezalel and Oholiab were called by name, filled with the divine Spirit, and inspired to teach their crafts to others (Exod. 35:30–34).[16] The Spirit's presence in teaching ministries encourages all forms of creativity, just as Bezalel and his colleagues used a variety of creative arts in their work. It is also significant to note that Bezalel had colleagues in his teaching ministry—Oholiab and the Holy Spirit. Having a companion on the teaching journey, like on the road to Emmaus, makes all the difference.

The positive potential of the creative arts as used by Bezalel and Oholiab is contrasted with those used to create the golden calf. The golden calf became a focus for idolatry (Exod. 32) as the Israelites worshiped the creature instead of the creator (Rom. 1:25). The very real abuses of teaching influence were evident in the widely publicized incidents at Jonestown, Guyana, and Waco, Texas, where the false teachings of Jim Jones and David Koresh took on tragic dimensions. Warnings about false teachers and prophets are found in the Scriptures (Matt. 7:15; 24:11, 24; 2 Cor. 11:13; 2 Pet. 2:1; 1 John 4:1). A spiritual discernment of teaching and its arts is required to avoid false teaching.

As the temple of the Holy Spirit, the Christian church must have clarity regarding its vision, mission, and memory to teach effectively. This is apparent in observing the pattern of Matthew's Gospel, where Jesus' earthly teaching is organized into five blocks or curricula addressing the three themes of vision, mission, and memory:

5:1–7:27	*vision* for the ethics of participation in God's kingdom
10:1–42	directives for the *mission* outreach of the twelve disciples
13:1–52	a framework for the redemptive history or *memory* of God's kingdom
18:1–35	guidelines for *mission* inreach among the disciples
23:1–25:4	*vision* of God's coming kingdom[17]

The teaching ministry requires a coordinated effort like that outlined for the oversight of the tabernacle as found in the Old Testament books of Leviticus and Numbers. It also calls for repeated curricular themes such as the kingdom of God, which is present in the five units of teaching in Matthew's Gospel.

Throughout the history of the Christian church, the collective memory has affirmed an understanding of the church as *one, holy, catholic,* and *apostolic.* Each of these marks has implications for teaching and helps to discern between false and true teaching in the life of the church.

Being *one* implies that Christian teachers need to affirm the perspective of Ephesians 4:1–16 and to honor Jesus' prayer in John 17:20–21: "I ask not only on behalf of these, but also on behalf of those who will believe in me through their word, that they may all be one. As you, Father, are in me and I am in you, may they also be in us, so that the world may believe that you have sent me." The unity of the Spirit in the church requires teachers to consider and explore ecumenical relations that affirm basic Christian truths and purposes. Christians can recognize that God delights to use others with whom we may disagree theologically, and I thank God for that reality. They can also affirm the common denominator of Jesus Christ who transcends all denominational and theological divisions.

Being *holy* implies that Christian teachers need to affirm God's demands and standards of righteousness and justice that require reliance upon the righteousness imparted to us in Jesus Christ. Jesus also prayed in John 17:17–19: "Sanctify them in the truth; your word is truth. As you have sent me into the world, so I have sent them into the world. And for their sakes I sanctify myself, so that they also may be sanctified in truth." Holiness implies a dedication to God in all areas of life, not just those related to the educational setting. Teachers are called to identify areas where they have failed personally and corporately and to seek through confession and repentance God's remedies of forgiveness and cleansing. Speaking the truth in love requires honesty and integrity (see the discussion of sin and salvation in chapter 2). In addition, the Apostle Paul appealed to Christians in 1 Corinthians 3:16–17: "Do you not know that you are God's temple and that God's Spirit dwells in you? If anyone destroys God's temple, God will destroy that person. For God's temple is holy, and you are that temple." Holiness extends to the physical body as well as the body of Christ: "Or do you not know that your body is a temple of the Holy Spirit within you, which you have from God, and that you are not your own? For you were bought with a price; therefore glorify God in your body" (1 Cor. 6:19–20).[18]

Being *catholic* implies that Christian teachers seek to discern God's truth from a variety of sources as they strive for universal understanding among Christians past, present, and future. The search for universal connections and relationships requires that openness through dialogue be stretched to welcome voices marginalized in our history. It also requires that we recognize the limits of our personal or communal stance, maintaining teachable spirits even while teaching with authority.

Being *apostolic* implies that Christian teachers seek to be faithful to the teaching of Jesus' apostles and the roots of the Christian faith. Apostolic roots as found in the New Testament assure faithfulness to the Christian tradition. Reliance upon the person and work of the Holy Spirit is essential in teaching because the Spirit brings to remembrance Jesus' teachings and guides Christians in the truth (John 14:26; 16:13).

Exploring the three dominant images of the church as the people of God, the body of Christ, and the temple of the Holy Spirit has addressed the matter of ecclesiology. A necessary complement to this discussion is an exploration of missiology, which considers the church's mission in the world.

The Church's Mission in the World

The late missiologist Orlando Costas was fond of describing mission as the mother of theology.[19] From his perspective, missiology should precede any theological reflection and discussion. A perspective I would affirm is that mission and theology partner with education in fostering the response of the whole people of God to the call of Christ in the world.[20] The church's mission is patterned after God's mission in the world as revealed in the life of the Trinity. An emphasis upon mission assumes that Christians are seriously considering the situation of persons throughout the world and the state of creation itself. In Latin America, this entry point for consideration opts for anthropology over ecclesiology. In other words, the focus is not on the church itself but on human beings and their lives in society. The mission of the church is to raise up and humanize people and to be an advocate for the needs of humanity given the ever-present devaluation of life as God intended it.[21] For the Christian church, the fullness of humanity is found in Jesus Christ. This fullness does not negate his divinity but provides an entry point for understanding the human condition and the church's call in relation to that condition.

Before considering the contours of the church's mission in the world, Christian educators must grapple with the definition of mission itself. Gabriel Fackre distinguishes between the inreach and the outreach of the church. Preaching and teaching *(kerygma)*, service or care within *(diakonia)*, life together within *(koinonia)*, and worship *(leitourgia)* all denote the inreach, nurture, or ministry of the church. The corresponding outreach tasks are evangelism *(kerygma)*, social service and action without *(diakonia)*, life together without *(koinonia)*, and festival *(leitourgia)*.[22] Mission denotes the outreach of the church. I would add to Fackre's list the inreach and outreach dimension of advocacy *(propheteia)*. As inreach, advocacy calls for accountability and evaluation within the church itself in relation to the demands of the gospel for justice, peace, and reconciliation among Christians. Questions can be posed about the place of the *anawim* and their voice, representation, and power in church affairs. Advocacy as outreach calls for works and words of justice, peace, and reconciliation in the wider community and society. Advocacy along with service fulfills God's mission in the world. In general, advocacy calls for the correction of past injustice, the positive pursuit of present justice, and the prevention of future injustice.[23] What holds true for justice in terms of the past, present, and future also applies to peace and reconciliation. The particulars of mission are named, but the matter of definition remains.

The work of David Bosch provides helpful categories for defining mission. Bosch proposes the concept of "transforming mission," suggesting that mission can be understood as an activity that transforms reality and that mission itself is constantly in need of transformation. Bosch cites the wisdom of James Russell Lowell, who said, "New occasions teach new duties: time makes ancient good uncouth."[24]

One example of Bosch's insight is the changing description of the church's mission in the Book of Acts. Life among believers included the tasks of proclamation, community formation, and worship (Acts 2:42–47). However, the needs of the church shifted to place more emphasis upon the need of *diakonia* or service (Acts 6:1–7). Service was not stressed to the exclusion of other parts of the Christian mission, but one aspect of the mission had a specific point of urgency at a particular time in the life of the church. The emphasis of Christians upon being faithful to God in each particular context must be balanced with fulfilling the universal purposes of God and the common mission of God in the world.

Bosch's distinction between mission and missions helps to maintain the balance. Mission refers to *missio Dei*, God's mission. In mission, God is revealed as the one who loves the world. Mission is God's involvement in and with the world. Mission is the nature and activity of God that embraces both the church and the world. Mission is God's mission in which the church is called and privileged to participate. Mission celebrates the universal purposes of God for all of creation and humanity. A focus on mission celebrates the unity and universality of God's work in the world.

Missions, in contrast, are *missiones ecclesiae*, the missionary ventures of the church in particular contexts. Missions refer to forms related to specific times, places, or needs. Missions are expressions of the church's participation in the *missio dei*. Missions celebrate the faithful response of the whole people of God in each community of believers.[25] Bosch's distinctions of the particularity of missions cannot ignore the universality of missions. Orlando Costas captured the universality of mission by observing that the church exists for mission, exists to tell, do, be, and celebrate the gospel *(kerygma, diakonia, koinonia, leitourgia)*.[26] The one addition I make to Costas's vision comes in relation to advocacy *(propheteia)*, which is to promote the gospel.

Considering the threefold office of Jesus' earthly ministry enhances our understanding of the contours of mission in relation to teaching. Missiologist Guillermo Cook observed that Jesus Christ has redefined the roles of prophet, priest, and king as they were modeled in the Old Testament. Christ redefines the prophetic mission in terms of incarnation, living out God's values in the world. Christ redefines the priestly mission in terms of sacrificial love, which must also be conceived in terms of steadfast love (Hos. 6:6). Christ redefines the royal or political mission of the king in terms of service to God, humanity, and the entire creation.[27] Each of Cook's proposed redefinitions of the threefold office has implications for our teaching efforts as part of the church's mission. God's mission as teacher finds expression through the faithful efforts of those called to be teachers. The order of the threefold office follows the traditional naming of prophet, priest, and king to describe Jesus' mission in the world.

Prophetic Mission of Teaching

In relation to Jesus' prophetic office, teachers and students function as those who are to incarnate God's values in the classroom, various educational settings, and the wider community. They fulfill this mission in a number of ways. Teachers, in particular, are to model those understandings, behaviors, and qualities related to the subject area they teach. By modeling what they hope students will embrace, teachers can serve as mentors for those less experienced. They can also model teachable spirits in how they approach the content of their teaching. Through openness, teachers can initiate students in a fascination with and wonder of the content. In this prophetic office, educators are called to denounce those ways of thinking, feeling, and behaving that are contrary to the teaching process. By doing so, teachers care enough to confront issues, problems, and patterns that can lead to the destruction of mind, body, or spirit. Teachers must be willing to stand in the gap for their students. This does not assume that the teacher is the only one to determine how a particular subject is presented. In a postmodern setting, teachers are expected to identify options and to be explicit about how their particular interests, experiences, and commitments influence their approach.

The prophetic mission of teachers includes the place of advocacy. They must be willing to voice the concerns of the voiceless. In this effort, teachers are aware of the explicit, implicit, and null curricula that Elliot Eisner describes in *The Educational Imagination*. The *explicit curriculum* is what the stated foci and intended learnings identify. The *implicit curriculum* refers to what is caught rather than directly taught. The *null curriculum* is that which is not taught. In other words, the explicit curriculum focuses more on the stated content—the *what* and *how* of teaching; the implicit curriculum addresses the formation of persons—the *who* and *why* of teaching; and the null curriculum is disclosed by considering the wider context—the *where* and *when* of teaching.[28]

Prophetic mission in teaching calls for the reexamination of curricular choices in relation to those issues that are on God's heart. In evaluation, the opportunity exists to consider the fruits of teaching in relation to the fivefold task of the church. As identified in chapter 4, my work *Basics of Teaching for Christians* proposes five values corresponding to each of the five tasks of the church:

proclamation—truth
community formation—love

service—faith
advocacy—hope
worship—joy

Related to each pairing is a mission call to teachers that can become a basis for evaluation in terms of integrity, care, action, courage, and celebration.[29] These provide a basis for prophetic assessment in discerning whether God's values are incarnate in actual teaching practice. If not, an agenda for advocacy is set.

Priestly Mission of Teaching

The priestly mission of teaching embraces the call to care for the content, persons, and context of teaching.[30] Expressions of love are evident in the devotion of teachers to the preparation for teaching. Care for content involves thought, time, and creativity in crafting lessons that honor the subject matter. Care for persons involves a willingness to risk oneself in appropriate sharing of one's life as an encouragement for students to share aspects of their lives. Such sharing fosters a sense of community and interaction outside the classroom. Care for the context of teaching requires sensitivity to the immediate and wider educational settings, including the familial, institutional, communal, societal, and global connections that relate the classroom to life. Care is directly related to the two great commandments to love God with all of our hearts, souls, minds, and strength and to love our neighbors as ourselves (Matt. 22:37; Mark 12:30; Luke 10:27). Loving care finds expression in the attention given to the content, persons, and context of teaching, and it fulfills in part the two great commandments through the ministries of teaching. It gives expression to God working *through* those of us who teach.

Priestly mission in teaching calls for attention to the unique contours of shared content as it impacts the mental, affective, and behavioral dimensions of learning. Content must be made accessible to students, and their readiness to grapple with the material must be considered. The needs and interests of the participants along with their particular learning styles call for the care of teachers. Nevertheless, care for style cannot avoid the appropriate stretch teaching provides that can enable learners to embrace new styles and experiences. Teachers must also care enough to share the wisdom they have gained while facilitating the students' discovery of truth for themselves. In addition, care for teaching involves sensitivity to a variety of environmental factors, including temperature, comfort, movement, and aesthetic appeal. The host of educational factors to consider can readily overwhelm even the most experienced of teachers. This may too readily result in neglecting oneself as a teacher. Teachers must accept their distinctive callings, strengths, and weaknesses. Proper stewardship of a teaching gift involves discernment of one's particular calling and the unique combination of personal and spiritual characteristics each of us is given.

Royal Mission of Teaching

The use of "royal" is appropriate to honor the value of teaching in passing on a heritage to future generations, which is a high calling. This royal mission directly relates to the political realm of life. Politics can be defined as the art of keeping persons fully human as God intended. Cook's intent was to stress the place of service to God, humanity, and all creation in this royal mission of the Christian church.[31] Education itself can be viewed as slow-fuse politics that seeks transformation in the human condition, but not through legislative, executive, judicial, diplomatic, or military means. Rather, teaching appeals primarily to the minds of persons but also to their spirits, hearts, intents, and actions. This appeal embraces certain values for life and relationships with others. Teaching invites persons to consider new ways of seeing, appreciating, judging, and acting within the world from a hopeful perspective. Hope is engaged as they affirm points of continuity with the past and points of change for the future. For Christian teachers, hope is embraced when God is seen as being active in the world through a partnership with the church. As the church owns God's mission and purposes, transformation is possible in the lives of persons, families, communities, and the wider society. This requires careful discernment of God's agenda for the world and the movements of God's Spirit in the affairs of creation and re-creation. The royal mission also requires an openness to God working through the frailties of human persons and groups. Because of the realities of sin, dangers exist of reducing God's desires to those advocated by persons. Therefore, protest and renewal become essential elements in following after God in both political and educational affairs. The politics of education requires the full participation of diverse persons to assure a broad ownership of educational purposes along with the freedom to dissent. God reserves the right to use persons with whom I disagree. Thank God, for that reality serves to relativize my grand schemes.

A royal mission suggests that teaching for service be a priority in Christian education. It also suggests that the learning derived from service experiences be honored in teaching. Service involvement provides an occasion for transformation from the self-centered, consumer-oriented preoccupation of a global economy as experienced in the United States. In my setting, the opportunities that faculty and students have to travel on mission ventures foster service learning.

On a recent trip to China that included a delegation of nineteen individuals from Andover Newton Theological School, new appreciation was gained for God's work in growing churches and seminaries. A sense of commitment on the part of Chinese Christians was palpable even in light of the persecution of the Cultural Revolution. Individual preferences for service are transcended by the needs of the corporate church in terms of fulfilling God's purposes. The realities of a postdenominational church enable Christians to affirm the common denominator of Jesus Christ whose prayer for unity in John 17 takes on historical expression. Many challenges confront the Chinese church, but a sense of God's presence and promises accompanies our Chinese Christian sisters and brothers in their teaching ministries. Those of us who have been afforded the privilege of this trip are now to serve as witnesses and advocates in our teaching and sharing. This mission opportunity can be the "mother" of theology. Those who traveled can theologically reflect upon their learning and its significance for God's mission in the world. Orlando Costas first traveled to China in 1986 when he was the academic dean of Andover Newton Theological School. He returned hoping that faculty and students might one day travel to China to witness God's work. Orlando died in 1987 when he was at the peak of his career as a globally recognized missiologist. Fourteen years later, Orlando's hope was fulfilled in the delegation that traveled from Andover Newton to China.

Conclusion

The mention of hope provides Christians with perspective regarding God's future, which is the focus of chapter 6. This fifth chapter has sought to connect teaching to both ecclesiology and missiology. Its essential teaching is the following: God works *through* us in the teaching ministries of the church that extend God's mission in the world. The nature of that mission in the world today includes cross-cultural connections like the one emerging between Andover Newton and the Chinese church. Similar connections reflect the Galilean principle that Jesus incarnated in his teaching ministry and mission.

SIX

GOD BEYOND US: OUR FUTURE IN CHRISTIAN EDUCATION

Just as the Trinity is a mystery we cannot fathom, we return to appreciate the mystery of the divine in an unfolding future that invites us to trust and hope in God. The Trinity continues to be our teacher in the present age and in ages to come. God's future finds current expression in realized eschatology as the Christian church experiences grace in Jesus Christ. The Christian church also hopes for the "not yet" of the fullness of God's promised consummation in the second coming of Christ. Teaching for this future calls Christians to appreciate the past and address the present with renewed vision in relation to God's plans for the consummation.[1] In commenting on eschatology, Millard Erickson suggests that "the truths of eschatology should arouse in us watchfulness and alertness in expectation of the future. . . . We should study the Scripture intensively and watch developments in our world carefully, so that we may discern God's working."[2]

In order to concretely address the future, Christians must move past some of their particular eschatological controversies to consider a shared future beyond theological divides. Christian educators can address their educational calling while maintaining Christian distinctives because of a shared future with Christians globally and historically. The future of Christian education in the third millennium calls for theological grappling with eschatology and tentativeness in recognizing the place of mystery. Some approaches to eschatology have been brash in their effort to "dogmatically identify specific historical occurrences with biblical prophecy or predict when certain eschatological events will take place."[3] However, the task before me in this chapter is not to present an easily followed recipe for Christian education that assures a digestible response to anticipated changes in the third millennium. The preoccupation with the future in our current social climate may fail to discern essential points of continuity with previous millennia and to affirm the "already" of Christ's blessings. Christian believers in every time and place are called to discern points of continuity and change that will guide a faithful response to God's calling to make disciples and teach all that Jesus taught (Matt. 28:18–20). For Christians, a faithful response requires openness to the surprises that God the Spirit will bless us with in the third millennium.

Windows on the Future

In discussing the theological theme of the consummation, Dorothy and Gabriel Fackre propose peering through four windows to gain perspective. The four windows they propose are the resurrection of the dead, the return of Christ, the last judgment, and everlasting life.[4] In relation to each window, a number of educational implications are considered. These four windows provide the basis for future teaching ministries as Christians respond to the invitations God would have us to consider.

The Resurrection of the Dead

The resurrection of the dead as described most explicitly in 1 Corinthians 15 indicates the divine purpose fulfilled in the wholeness of persons restored as bodies and souls in relationship with God and all creation. This resurrection completes the salvation offered in Christ as discussed in chapter 2 of this work. Education that exclusively stresses the mind while neglecting the body and relationships with God and all creation is incomplete. Reconciliation and healing apply to all that God intends for humanity as embodied in life. Christ's resurrection body provides a glimpse of what God intends for redeemed humanity (1 Cor. 15:20).[5] Christian educators ought to consider the embodied nature of their ministries in relation to setting and the physical needs of persons. If the body is the temple of the Holy Spirit, then rest, nutrition, and exercise are important considerations both inside and outside the classroom or ministry context. Respect and stewardship of the body include confronting destroyers of the body in the wider society. It also calls for ministries of advocacy and service to those deprived of bodily necessities.

In relation to resurrection, the Apostle Paul makes a helpful connection to an underlying purpose of Christian education in Philippians 3:10–11: "I want to know Christ and the power of his resurrection and the sharing of his sufferings by becoming like him in his death, if somehow I may attain the resurrection from the dead." To know Christ and make him known is, I trust, an essential element of the implicit curriculum in Christian education. Though we may shy away from suffering and sharing with Jesus in his death, the promise of life awaits all who seek to follow Christ. The power of Jesus' resurrection makes possible transformation and new life in the face of death. Transformation is evident in the raising of a spiritual body in place of a physical body and the gift of immortality in place of mortality. The ultimate source for transformation is found in the victory of Jesus' actual resurrection from the dead and the promise of our future resurrection. Jesus' words as recorded in John's Gospel provide reassurance for our life in the interim between this age and the age to come:

> Jesus said to them, "I am the bread of life. Whoever comes to me will never be hungry, and whoever believes in me will never be thirsty. But I said to you that you have seen me and yet do not believe. Everything that the Father gives me will come to me, and anyone who comes to me I will never drive away; for I have

come down from heaven, not to do my own will, but the will of him who sent me. And this is the will of him who sent me, that I should lose nothing of all that he has given me, but raise it up on the last day. This is indeed the will of my Father, that all who see the Son and believe in him may have eternal life; and I will raise them up on the last day."(John 6:35–40)

The Return of Christ

The return of Christ, which is itself a mystery not subject to our projected schemes for fulfillment, provides a hope for Christians (Mark 13:32). Christ's second coming complements the teaching of his first coming (see chapter 3) with a promised eternity of teaching offered to a new humanity and new creation that God will bring to fruition. First John describes this hope in explicit terms:

And now, little children, abide in him, so that when he is revealed we may have confidence and not be put to shame before him at his coming. If you know that he is righteous, you may be sure that everyone who does right has been born of him. See what love the Father has given us, that we should be called children of God; and that is what we are. The reason the world does not know us is that it did not know him. Beloved, we are God's children now; what we will be has not yet been revealed. What we do know is this: when he is revealed, we will be like him, for we will see him as he is. And all who have this hope in him purify themselves, just as he is pure. (1 John 2:28–3:3)

The hope of Christ's second coming is a motivation for holy living in terms of how Christians represent their Lord and Savior in this life. As children of God, Christians are called to righteous and holy living. As recipients of God's grace, forgiveness, salvation, and adoption, Christians have confidence in this life and in the life to come by abiding in Christ. Those who follow Jesus in this life look forward to his appearing as the ultimate encounter. This hope adds a sense of joy to the Christian journey and its fulfillment in seeing Jesus. Jesus, who gave his life to restore our lives in relationship to God, is embraced as beloved. This was the joyful experience of Mary Magdalene in

John 20:11–18 (see chapter 3). Seeing Jesus as he is was possible for Mary in response to his recognizing her by name and his knowing her at the very depth of her being. This is Jesus as the Master Teacher for all eternity. Through his living and dying, he instructs us about what is of ultimate importance in life. At its best, Christian education seeks to enhance a fullness of life, death, and life after death for all of humanity and creation. This potential finds fulfillment in Christ's second coming to complete what was begun in his earthly ministry. It extends through history in the mission of the Christian church by the presence and power of the Holy Spirit.

The Last Judgment

The last judgment provides an ultimate basis for accountability and responsibility in human and educational affairs. Sin and salvation (see chapter 2) play out their eternal consequences in line with the continuing ministry of the Holy Spirit (see chapter 4). God's standards of holiness, righteousness, freedom, and justice provide the final evaluation for human efforts. Matthew 23:1–25:46 provides a concise unit known as the Olivet Discourse in which Jesus teaches on eschatology and the nature of the last judgment. Matthew's Gospel as a whole has been insightfully considered a teaching manual for the early church, with Jesus' specific teaching on the last judgment found in Matthew 25:31–46. The description of the sheep and goats and of their final separation is suggestive of the ultimate consequences for the righteous and wicked. Jesus is to be seen in the faces of the hungry, thirsty, strangers, naked, sick, and prisoners whom we encounter in daily life. Eternal life and eternal punishment are the consequences for the actions of all nations in being gathered before the Son of Man. Those gathered for judgment are "the same group that the disciples are commissioned to baptize and teach according to the last words of Matthew's Gospel. The judgment scene in chapter 25 thus looks forward to the close of the age and assumes the completion of the universal task of 'teaching the nations.'"[6]

What teachers and learners pattern in their times of assessment and evaluation take on ultimate consequences in light of God's intentions and purposes. The values God has modeled for humanity and most explicitly revealed in Jesus Christ are the terms for judgment. God's loving provision for human failure is the gift of the Son to those who will accept him. For the task of teaching, Christians are assured that Jesus will be with us always to the end of the age (Matt. 28:20).

The remedy for human sin as discussed in chapter 2 is the complete salvation Christ makes available. This salvation also applies to teachers and our shortcomings. The educational issues under discussion currently include a concern for outcome assessment and accountability for results. Teachers and students are evaluated based on the outcomes identified prior to teaching. The extent to which the realities of personal and corporate human sin fit the proposed formulas needs to be raised. At times educators take the arrogant stance that their efforts will effect learning regardless of the investment or commitment of the persons involved. Reserving a place for the ministry of the Holy Spirit and recognizing sin in both teachers and students is crucial in any proposals for causality by Christian educators. The reality of ultimate judgment and the penultimate judgments of educational evaluation require Christian teachers to consider their ministry of reconciliation as described in 2 Corinthians 5:11–6:12.[7]

Everlasting Life

Everlasting life fulfills God's original intentions that have been diverted through the fall of humanity and all of creation. Christ's life, death, and resurrection make eternal life possible for fallen humanity. The ministry and mission of the Christian church as described in chapter 5 find their ultimate fulfillment in God's gracious gift. For Christians there is no greater love than what Jesus has sewn in the fabric of human flesh and blood. His gift makes possible a quality of life that Christians long for in the kingdom Jesus has already brought into being. Jesus' earthly ministry brought the firstfruits of abundant life through his reign in the hearts and lives of his followers. The full embrace of that new and higher life awaits the consummation but provides perspective for our entire earthly journey. Everlasting life provides a basis for all education that seeks to enhance and foster life this side of eternity. Sharing the wells from which eternal life springs is what Jesus promised to the Samaritan woman at the well and to all who believe (John 4:14; 7:37–38). This living water is what Christian educators can offer to a thirsty humanity and a groaning creation (Rom. 8:18–25).

In describing everlasting life, Dorothy and Gabriel Fackre draw upon biblical images to outline the "final reconciliation of all things" in terms of reconciling humanity with God, reconciling human nature with supernature, and reconciling nature itself.[8] The final reconciliation of humanity with God described in Revelation 4 and 5 results in resounding worship of God and the Lamb who are worthy of glory, honor, power, blessing, wealth, wisdom, and might (Rev. 4:11; 5:9–14). If our ultimate destiny focuses on such worship, reverence, awe, wonder, and adoration before God and Christ, the central focus of our educational efforts should relate to worship and celebration before our Triune God. All of life should be viewed as an act of worship, including our educational life. To me this suggests the need to place worship as the center of my five-task educational model.

The reconciliation of human nature with supernature is described in Revelation as "all the estranged shall dwell in unity in the city of God."[9] The biblical record recounts the historical progression from life in the Garden of Eden to life in the Holy City. The ultimate goal of human history is to restore relationship with the Triune God that was lost in the garden through human freedom and choice. The restoration of relationship is realized by dwelling in the city where God is found. "Powers as well as persons come together, finally giving obedience and praise to their Maker and Redeemer" (Rev. 7:11; 21:10–11).[10]

The reconciliation of nature is vividly described in Revelation 21:1 and 22:1–2:

> Then I saw a new heaven and a new earth; for the first heaven and the first earth had passed away, and the sea was no more. . . . Then the angel showed me the river of the water of life, bright

as crystal, flowing from the throne of God and of the Lamb through the middle of the street of the city. On either side of the river is the tree of life with its twelve kinds of fruit, producing its fruit each month; and the leaves of the tree are for the healing of the nations.[11]

Persistent global ecological concerns are worthy of the efforts of Christian educators in light of both the creation and God's ultimate purposes in reconciliation (Rom. 8:18–25).

Peering through these four theological windows on the future, I discern three continuing educational forms that will serve the Christian church in its teaching ministries. The three forms are the educational trinity, the five-task model, and the Chalcedonian form or grammar. These forms have been described in earlier chapters. The two forms of the educational trinity and Chalcedonian form were made most explicit in chapter 3 with the discussion of Jesus' example as the norm for Christian teaching in the past, present, and future. These forms emerge from taking seriously the fact that Jesus is the "pioneer and perfecter of our faith" (Heb. 12:2). I argue that Jesus also holds this essential role in relation to the thought and practice of Christian teachers.

Chalcedonian form in relation to Jesus' teaching ministry recognizes the interplay of various elements in his person. Jesus was both human and divine and in his incarnation limited his divine power and prerogatives to better communicate with and model a full humanity (Phil. 2:5–11). Those who follow Jesus in teaching ministries also struggle with both/and tensions.

The broad mission assigned to Jesus' followers, organized and empowered by the very Spirit of Christ at Pentecost, ought to relate to the various teaching ministries engaged by Christians. The five-task model is one form to describe that mission and see the connections across the five tasks. The fulfillment of these tasks requires the gifts and empowerment of the Holy Spirit and the cooperative efforts of God's people across the generations and across time with eternity in view. An eternal perspective suggests that the ultimate destiny for humanity and all of creation is to be in relationship with our Triune God.

The very nature of God as Trinity as discussed in chapter 1 provides a theological theme that relates to how we view education for present and future teaching ministries. My proposal of an educational trinity that considers the content, persons, and context of Christian education is the first perennial form for consideration in projecting beyond the present realities of Christian education.

An Educational Trinity

The Trinity is the organizing theological theme for this entire work. It applies to the future of Christian education in considering an educational trinity. The content, persons, and context of Christian education must receive careful attention in future educational ministries. I define education as the process of sharing content with persons in the context of their community and society. Christian education is differentiated from general education by the extent to which it fulfills the distinct Christian purposes as suggested by the five-task model. The theology of the Trinity explored in chapter 1 and Jesus' exemplary teaching ministry analyzed in chapter 3 support the continuing applicability of my educational trinity of content, persons, and context for the future. Historical battles over educational philosophy have divided educators who tend to stress only one or two poles of the educational trinity. Such choices have resulted in various forms of reductionism that have plagued the church and her teaching ministries.[12] A holistic vision for the present and future requires that attention be given to each of the three educational elements of content, persons, and context. This is our challenge in following the example of Jesus as Master Teacher for all time and eternity. We can learn from the philosophical battles of the past and avoid their reductionisms of practice that fail to balance the content, persons, and context of education.

Content

The content of Christian education in the future cannot be formulated without adequate attention to both the persons and context of teaching. The valid concerns for biblical, theological, and liturgical literacy in future Christian teaching ministries must be complemented by consideration of the persons participating in Christian education and their wider communal and societal context. In their preparation for teaching, Christians need to consider who their audiences are and what their life situations may be.[13] Awareness and analysis of individual students provide some insights for what they may already know about a particular subject. Insights are also possible regarding how the participants themselves are resources for each other in the educational event and how to foster dialogue that draws upon what they can offer. Too often, the experience and wisdom of participants are not accessed, and mutual edification is thereby limited. Learning is not limited to times when the teacher is active and the participants are receptive. The receptivity of the teacher can model an openness to others, vulnerability, and a teachable spirit. However, in stressing the persons of the participants, a danger is ignoring the potential wisdom and expertise that the teacher offers. To reduce teaching to the exclusive facilitation of learning limits teachers' calling and authority and Jesus' example of one who taught with authority.[14]

It is important to note that content is not limited to the intellect. A holistic understanding of learning requires attention to emotion, intention, physical activity, and character and spiritual formation.[15] The Christian affirmation of the resurrection of the dead gives honor to whole persons. This wider consideration also requires attention to the context for teaching. Educators must construct a bridge between the teaching setting and the world outside. Here is where teachers must raise the matter of the transfer of learning into life. One immediate way to address this gap is to include life issues and community concerns as part of the actual teaching agenda. A danger teachers must consider, though, is trying to fit students into the existing expectations and roles for persons outside the classroom and neglecting the place of transformation. Some aspects of teaching involve training individuals for predictable responsibilities and real-life functions in the wider world. However, the additional element of a transformative purpose is to equip persons for the unpredictable and for creative responses to challenges that have yet to be encountered in the community and society. This requires more than tailoring teaching to easily stated outcomes and suggests the need for creative exploration of questions and problems that are not subject to easy solutions or quick fixes. All three poles of the educational trinity call for our consideration in future teaching.

Persons

The often-proposed solution to Christian education preoccupied with content is to advocate a learner-centered approach that promises to solve all the problems of boredom. Active engagement of learners promises to assure teachers that motivation will be high and positive feelings fostered. I value the active participation and enthusiasm of students and attempt to tap into their interests and imagination in educational events. However, the insights of Abraham Heschel have served to warn me of the dangers in a total preoccupation with participants. Heschel's first warning comes in his wisdom regarding thinking itself: "Thinking without roots will bear flowers but no fruits."[16] In teaching encounters, most persons focus on the present and future to the relative neglect of the past. Exceptions can always be cited to this tendency, especially with older adults. It is often the role of the teacher to discern and share the roots of thinking that serve to sustain persons and communities over time. The noteworthy exception of older adults suggests the need for younger generations to avail themselves of the wisdom older adults can offer regarding the roots of faith and life for all of us regardless of age. In relation to content, this suggests the essential need for teachers to share transformative and sustaining content that is too often forgotten.

The second insight from Heschel relates to his warning about the exclusive focus on needs that is associated with person-centered teaching. Focusing on needs can result in a total disregard for God's demands that transcend the fulfilling of self-defined needs. In relation to educational life, this results in a tyranny of needs, according to Heschel.[17] Christian teachers must evaluate persons' needs in the light of distortions that a society or culture may perpetuate. Heschel's concerns should not result in dismissing genuine human needs. Rather, the concern is to raise critical awareness regarding what needs may be used to guide teaching and what alternatives teachers can suggest to liberate persons from the tyranny of needs in light of God's design for human and created life. Such discernment is possible through the sharing of transformative content and the reflective consideration of how Jesus posed questions to his followers.

Context

The significant changes in community and society and their impact upon the various generations draw the attention of teachers today. The philosophical and cultural shifts identified with postmodernity invite educational innovation (see appendix). As Christians, we have not chosen the time of our earthly journeys in terms of human history. In his teaching ministry, Jesus demonstrated a careful reading of the context and skillfully fashioned the truths he disclosed and encouraged others to discover. He made creative use of contemporary objects and events to reveal spiritual wisdom of timeless quality. The danger in our teaching efforts is becoming context-bound without the facility or faculty to see beyond our immediate setting. This leads to a contextualism that fails to learn from others and to see new possibilities of what God can bring to pass. Our God beyond us provides a transcendent perspective as an alternative to contextual boundedness. Here the transformative content of the gospel and the words and insights of a prophetic voice that stands on the margins of the community or society may only be ignored at great peril.

Our immediate context can be so restricted that no new light or truth can penetrate. The consequence is that our teaching rehearses old scripts with joyless results. One recent example of this comes from an educational setting where the presence and effectiveness of single persons is questioned. One wonders whether Jesus as a single adult would gain any access in this setting. Too often difference is interpreted as deficit in an educational context where critical questions are squelched and conformity is stressed. In some teaching contexts, persons are not respected where their distinctives conflict with or contradict communal or societal norms. An exclusive focus on the context of teaching can ignore content that intentionally stretches the community or the interaction with persons who are viewed as other. Learning from "the other," whoever that may be, provides an occasion to see from the perspective of what is often forgotten or ignored in our particular community or society. Contemporary life with its global connections calls for an openness to the other that need not threaten individual or community identity. Encountering the other can better enable me to face the other that resides within myself.

Balance

The preceding discussion of content, persons, and context indicates the need for a balanced approach to future Christian teaching that honors the educational trinity. The educational trinity calls us to attend to content, persons, and context in ways that do not reduce our focus to just one of those essential elements in educational planning and design. Balance is a particular challenge in a time of quick fixes and practical outcomes that fail to wrestle with the wider issues that will affect generations to come. The way to maintain balance is dialogue across philosophical and cultural differences, to embrace a willingness to risk change, and to sustain relationships and continuity even in the face of conflict. Amid increasing diversity, the search for common ground and unity requires the commitment of time to develop trust, respect, and civility in the outworking of a public theology that sees all persons as created in God's image and worthy of respect and care.

In a public dialogue, what distinguishes Christian education from public or general education may be a concern. From my perspective, a five-task model distinguishes Christian education because it connects education with the perennial purposes or tasks of the Christian church. The church has a mission in the world as those sent and empowered by God to make a difference.

A Five-Task Model

Distinct from the concept in chapter 3 that identifies one dominant and all-encompassing paradigm, a five-task model should be considered alongside other approaches to Christian education. The five tasks I identify to guide Christian educators also apply to educators from diverse traditions who seek to effectively teach in the third millennium. The five tasks, as previously noted, are proclamation, community formation, service, advocacy, and worship.[18]

The five-task model can be envisioned as a mandala (a circle enclosing a square) with worship at its center, and proclamation, community formation, service, and advocacy as the four equidistant points of the square on the outer circle. The four complementary points of the square on the mandala can be connected to form a central cross that runs vertically and horizontally. The circle itself is suggestive of a face and denotes wholeness. The theological significance of this symbol is that we encounter the face of God portrayed as a circle in the cross of Jesus Christ. Jesus becomes the "face of God for us."[19] Joy-centered worship of God is realized through suffering, the suffering of Christ's cross. Samuel Solivan suggests that suffering is a theological key to move beyond the particularities of race, class, and gender in embracing the universality of Jesus Christ for humanity and all of creation.[20] In the face of Jesus, all of humanity can find meaning and salvation, regardless of their roots. One of the insights Paul shared with the Christians at Philippi was that the goal of knowing Christ and the power of his resurrection included "the sharing of his sufferings by becoming like him in his death" (Phil. 3:10). The human situation includes the realities of suffering. God's remedy for suffering is found in the person and work of Jesus Christ.

I have identified five issues that will affect religious education in the third millennium: changing technologies, global interdependence, patterns of social interaction, the place of knowledge versus wisdom, and the matter of time perspective.[21] Each of these five issues relates to one of the tasks God has called the Christian church to fulfill this side of eternity.

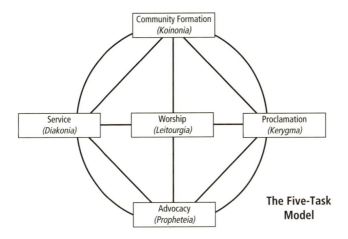

The Five-Task Model

The issue of changing technologies relates to the task of proclamation and the call to present the gospel with integrity through new forms and media. The issue of global interdependence relates to the task of community formation that transcends national and cultural borders. Consciousness of the global community calls for a response of care and love for all of humanity and creation. Patterns of social interaction beyond isolated individualism relates to the task of service. The connection between social interaction and service poses the question, Whom do I serve?

The issue of knowledge versus wisdom lies at the center of educational thought and practice. What knowledge or wisdom is most revered and awed? Is human wisdom or God's wisdom most sought after and celebrated? The greatest source of joy and fulfillment is found in God's wisdom incarnated in Jesus Christ (Col. 2:2–3). The Book of James compares two kinds of wisdom (James 3:13–18). Godly wisdom is "pure, then peaceable, gentle, willing to yield, full of mercy and good fruits, without a trace of partiality or hypocrisy" (v. 17). By comparison, ungodly wisdom is described as earthly, unspiritual, devilish, envious, selfish, and leading to disorder and wickedness (vv. 15–16). For those of us who lack godly wisdom, James suggests a remedy: "If any of you is lacking in wisdom, ask God, who gives to all generously and ungrudgingly, and it will be given you" (1:5).

The final issue of time perspective relates to the task of advocacy. What is most forgotten in our preoccupation with the present and future is a connection with the past and the importance of historical roots that ground and sustain educational ministry. Continuity with the past and the underlying sources of life with the Triune God calls for the appropriation of enduring forms.[22] The possibility of enduring forms is questioned from the perspective of postmodern philosophical and cultural trends. Nevertheless, these forms have continued vitality for teaching in the present and future.

In relation to the five-task model, it is essential that each Christian ministry evaluate its vision, mission, purpose, and practice with regard to those given and gifted to the church.[23] They are given in terms of calling and commission, and they are gifted in terms of the Spirit's empowerment and enablement. Each community or ministry has its particular strengths and calling, but connection with the eternal purposes of God and the nature of God's mission provides clarity and direction.[24] Also, the danger of disconnected and fragmented efforts across both church and parachurch ministries is conceptually avoided by seeing the relationship with God's universal mission and eternal purposes. The particular character of God's mission is impacted by the multicultural, religious, and ideological diversities of our time. The five-task model invites us to transcend our exclusive preoccupation with local or parochial concerns. In relation to that challenge, the Chalcedonian form of Jesus' teaching ministry has much to offer Christian educators in their future ministries.

Chalcedonian Form

Chalcedonian form finds expression in the need for both huddling and mixing in Christian education. Jesus modeled both intentional huddling with God and his people and mixing with others without losing his identity and vitality. By becoming human, Jesus huddled and identified with humanity (John 1:14), and though laying aside some of the power and prerogatives of his divinity (Phil. 2:5–11), he mixed without confusion or diminution the divine life of the Trinity with his human life. Chalcedonian form affirms the "indissoluble differentiation, inseparable unity, and indestructible order" that characterizes the relationship between the divine and human in Jesus.[25] By embracing and huddling humanity with all of its suffering, Jesus redeemed humanity and all of creation by mixing without dissolution the potentialities of trinitarian life in his offer of salvation. These blessings are made available through his life, death, resurrection, and ascension. A new unity of life and purpose becomes possible as priority is given to God's perspective and initiation in all human experiences and endeavors including education. Jesus' first-century Galilean life balances the huddling of his Jewish identity with the mixing of his multicultural context. As explored in chapter 3, Jesus' life sustains the Chalcedonian grammar and models the Galilean principle. Huddling in his Jewish identity affirms local particularity, while mixing in Galilee affirms multicultural universality made possible through his divine nature as sustained by the Holy Spirit.[26]

The recent work of Klaus Issler raises a crucial question for Christian educators following Jesus' model: How human was or is Jesus? In response to this question, Issler proposes three possible answers:

1. Jesus walked and talked using *primarily* his own divine powers, with very little use of his own human powers.
2. Jesus walked and talked using *mostly* his human powers, supplemented by the occasional use of his divine powers.
3. Jesus walked and talked using *solely* his own human powers, without any recourse to his own divine powers, but relying on the divine power of the Holy Spirit.[27]

Issler opts for the third response and concludes that Jesus "lived his life as an example for us solely with his own human abilities, not resorting to his own divine powers, but relying moment by moment on the supernatural power of the Holy Spirit."[28]

In relation to Chalcedonian form, Jesus' teaching models a priority given to his relationship with and reliance upon the Holy Spirit, though his very person fully unified both divine and human natures. His incarnation came at a cost he was willing to accept in accomplishing God's purposes. Jesus accepted this cost because of his love for humanity. In his reliance upon the Spirit, he provides a model for human teachers who need the presence and power of the Holy Spirit to engage in transformative teaching. Therefore, it is essential that Christian teachers, through prayer and other spiritual disciplines, discern the leading and power of the Spirit in their ministries. Christian educators must be guided by the order of loves suggested in the two great commandments.

Huddling suggests the need for relationships with persons of like mind and experience. However, huddling requires the complementary mixing where spiritual insights connect with real-life situations in a diversity of factors and perspectives. In the contemporary world, that diversity includes religious, cultural, ideological, and philosophical differences. In order to navigate diverse elements in a sea of pluralism, Christian educators often serve as sentinels on the walls of the faith community. A sentinel is one who lovingly keeps vigil, who guards persons, property, community, or institution. A sentinel is often the gatekeeper, deciding who will gain entrance and influence. One educational watchword I suggest for the future in the light of Chalcedonian form is to both huddle and mix, thereby embracing the Galilean principle modeled by Jesus.

A passage of Scripture that describes the responsibility of discernment and watchfulness is Ezekiel 33:1–9, where Ezekiel is identified as Israel's sentry:

> The word of the LORD came to me: O Mortal, speak to your people and say to them, If I bring the sword upon a land, and the people of the land take one of their number as their sentinel; and if the sentinel sees the sword coming upon the land and blows the trumpet and warns the people; then if any who hear the sound of the trumpet do not take warning, and the sword comes and takes them away, their blood shall be upon their own heads. They heard the sound of the trumpet and did not take warning; their blood shall be upon themselves. But if they had taken warning, they would have saved their lives. But if the sentinel sees the sword coming and does not blow the trumpet, so that the people are not warned, and the sword comes and takes any of

them, they are taken away in their iniquity, but their blood I will require at the sentinel's hand.

So you, mortal, I have made a sentinel for the house of Israel; whenever you hear a word from my mouth, you shall give them warning from me. If I say to the wicked, "O wicked ones, you shall surely die," and you do not speak to warn the wicked to turn from their ways, the wicked shall die in their iniquity, but their blood I will require at your hand. But if you warn the wicked to turn from their ways, and they do not turn from their ways, the wicked shall die in their iniquity, but you will have saved your life.

The ministry of teaching as it relates to the future can be compared with the work of a sentry or sentinel. The sentry duty of teaching is a matter of stewardship of God's grace (1 Pet. 4:1–11). James 3:1 emphasizes that responsibility: "Not many of you should become teachers, my brothers and sisters, for you know that we who teach will be judged with greater strictness." The next verse in that passage points out that we all make many mistakes. Certainly, God's grace applies to teaching as to all areas of life, and "love covers a multitude of sins" (1 Pet. 4:8). Nevertheless, teachers need the divine wisdom of the Holy Spirit to effectively minister with discernment and watchfulness and invest our lives in current and future generations. Psalm 127:1 provides a needed reminder for those who serve as sentinels: "Unless the LORD guards the city, the guard keeps watch in vain." In addition, faithful teachers are encouraged to wait upon and watch for God in their personal lives: "My soul waits for the Lord more than those who watch for the morning" (Ps. 130:6). Guarding the future also calls for watchfulness and stewardship in relation to particular church communities. My personal experience with a group of church educators provides one example.

In 1996, a number of colleagues and I participated in a conference to address the future of Christian educators. The final document from the conference identifies seven mandates for the revival of Christian education: be relational versus institutional; be relevant; have strong leadership; have story at its center; be done in partnership; be innovative; and have clarity of

mission and vision.[29] After reviewing the conference document
and engaging in further Bible study, I compared the seven mandates with the messages to the seven churches in Revelation 2
and 3. Revelation is the New Testament book Christians consider when exploring the future. It throbs with a consciousness
of the living Christ as present in the life of local churches. Jesus
is described as the Lord of the churches in Revelation. In studying Revelation, I discovered a remarkable parallel between each
of the mandates and the messages recorded for the seven
churches. I note each parallel in the following pages. While
reflecting upon these mandates, I was also struck by the contemporary application of the messages given to the seven
churches of Revelation. Watchfulness calls us to discern the presence of the risen Lord in the life of Christian churches and in
various ministries today and in the future.

A significant insight I gained from the conference's envi-
sioning work is that to address the future of Christian education, Christians need to start, continue, and end with biblical
revelation. This lesson addresses the question, How can persons of faith respond to the invitations of the third millennium in ways that are faithful to Christian traditions? The
conference started by considering the biblical passages of
Deuteronomy 6:1–9, 20–25, Luke 5:27–39, and Revelation
21:1–5. These passages were chosen to emphasize our past
tradition, the present indwelling of the Holy Spirit, and our
hope for the future. From this biblical starting point, I discerned a need to return to biblical sources for further reflections on educational thought and practice. After exploring the
biblical foundations, conference participants formed small
groups and inductively explored a number of educational case
studies. The seven mandates sought to summarize their find-
ings and provide direction for the future. Writing this chapter enabled me to search for additional light from the Scriptures to gain perspective on the future proposed by the
conference. Reliance upon the Scriptures calls for biblical and
theological reflection before, during, and following educational planning. The Scriptures serve to reveal or disclose our
cherished perspectives—and us—while we read them. Both
inductive and deductive educational approaches gain per-

spective in wrestling with the biblical record. My discussion below indicates the value of a return to biblical sources following an inductive approach, even one that explicitly began with biblical study and foundations.

Ephesus: Be Relational versus Institutional

The message to the church in Ephesus is to remember their first love and to restore their relationship with God (Rev. 2:1–7). This relationship is modeled in the Trinity (see chapter 1) and is made available through Christ to all his followers. In the case of the church at Ephesus, this called for repentance to restore the relationship. Repentance is necessary because of the presence of sin (see chapter 2).

In relation to Christian education, a deep hunger for the experience of positive relationships exists in the wider culture. Educational offerings provide an occasion for persons to develop intimacy with small groups of others seeking to learn about and follow Jesus. The Christian church offers an opportunity to develop a sense of community across the generations within an age-segregated society. Teachers can be equipped to develop bonds of caring beyond times of formal education by fostering nonformal and informal learning. We live in an institutional world, yet within those institutions caring relationships make all the difference in sustaining life as God intended it.

Smyrna: Be Relevant

The message to the church in Smyrna (Rev. 2:8–11) is to be fruitful even in the face of suffering and death. Relevance in today's world often calls for naming and identifying with the suffering of others. In the case of the believers in Smyrna, their own suffering served as a bridge to others. Popular wisdom suggests that a suffering shared is half the suffering, and a joy shared is twice the joy.

Hosts of issues confront persons in their personal and public lives. Christian education provides an opportunity to discuss those issues in relationship to questions of faith. Active learning can foster application of Christian virtues and values to where and how persons live, move, and have their beings. The press for relevance can encourage exploration of deep wells that can sustain fullness in life with its suffering and joy.

Pergamum: Have Strong Leadership

The message to the church in Pergamum (Rev. 2:12–17) recounts the problems of following false leadership and teaching as exemplified in Balaam and Balak. The implied alternative is to identify and support strong leaders who can make positive differences in all ministries, including those of Christian education.

In most churches, the need for leadership development is a high priority in the future educational agenda. Following the example of Jesus as explored in chapter 3, the ministries of mentoring and discipling are key to sustaining a vital faith community. Identifying a variety of leadership gifts and abilities is the first step in equipping persons to serve as the church is both gathered and scattered in the world.

Thyatira: Have Story at Its Center

The message to the church in Thyatira (Rev. 2:18–29) relates to the seduction of an alternative faith story, the teaching of Jezebel, which calls for participating in sexual immorality and eating food sacrificed to idols. These alternatives serve as secrets in the story line disclosed to those initiated into the false teaching. The clear and true story of the gospel provides the necessary remedy.

Christian education can be viewed as fostering the intersection of Christian story with both personal and communal stories. Narrative approaches to theology have fostered a renewal of storytelling as a primary method for Christian teaching.[30] The telling, retelling, and reshaping of faith stories with others provides a bond for Christian community across the generations.

Sardis: Be Done in Partnership

The message to the church in Sardis (Rev. 3:1–6) relates to a partnership of those properly clothed. Those dressed in white are properly clothed and unspotted. They are true and reliable partners who can equally share in the Christian mission.

The failures of individualistic approaches to life indicate the need for developing cooperation and collaboration. Leadership that fosters growth embraces patterns of partnership as modeled in the earthly ministry of Jesus Christ and the missionary outreach of the early Christian church (Acts 11:19–30). The pattern for emulation is the Trinity, which has served as a theological touchstone throughout this work. The key partner for the Christian church is the Holy Spirit. Current interests in spirituality need to foster relationships with the Spirit.

Philadelphia: Be Innovative

The message to the church in Philadelphia (Rev. 3:7–13) identifies an open door of opportunity (innovation) and a holding on to what is already possessed (continuity). The pillar in the temple (continuity) is complemented by a new name (innovation or change). A balance of innovation and continuity is required to advance the future educational ministries of the Christian church.

C. S. Lewis observed that growth does not emerge just from change, but from a discerning combination of continuity and change. The failure to consider all forms of innovation results in stagnation and the loss of vitality. Persons were fashioned with tremendous creative potential that needs to be channeled in ways that glorify God. In a culture preoccupied with images, imagination holds the potential for either illumination or illusion. Innovation must maintain its moorings with Christian theological orthodoxy in order to remain faithful.

Laodicea: Have Clarity of Vision and Mission

The message to the church in Laodicea (Rev. 3:14–22) relates to lukewarmness. Being lukewarm results in a lack of clarity and conviction regarding vision and mission. It also assumes a self-sufficiency and self-complacency that does not issue in commitment and action. Repentance and earnestness are required to restore purpose in vision and mission.

The educational challenge in relation to both vision and mission is for Christian educators to pose foundational questions that enable Christians to gain clarity regarding God's calling and purposes. Once clarity is gained, the corresponding challenge is to foster sustained commitment and endurance for fruitful Christian ministry and mission in the world.

The seven mandates for the future of Christian education as interpreted through Revelation 2 and 3 and my personal experiences are merely suggestions. Each Christian educator must filter them through the demands and requirements of her or his particular tradition and setting. All Christian traditions affirm a God and Christ and Spirit who are alive and eager to bring a reviving presence into all of life, including Christian education. This is the invitation of the third millennium for Christian educators and all those who have a living faith in Jesus the Christ.[31]

God's ultimate revelation awaits the second coming of Jesus Christ. The mandates for the seven churches in Revelation anticipate the presence of the Alpha and Omega: "Look! He is coming with the clouds; every eye will see him, even those who pierced him; and on his account all the tribes of the earth will wail" (Rev. 1:7). The immediate future grows pale in light of the eternal reign promised in the second coming of Jesus Christ and the teaching that will occur in his presence. For the writer of Revelation, that future involves the coming of a New Jerusalem (Rev. 21–22). God's purposes that began in a garden are consummated in the coming of the Holy City.

Conclusion

In this final chapter, I have explored Christian education beyond our present realities. In response to the future's invitations, I propose three forms of continuing viability for Christian education: (1) an educational trinity that considers the content, persons, and context of education; (2) a five-task model of proclamation, community formation, service, advocacy, and worship; and (3) a Chalcedonian form related to the educational formula of "huddle and mix." These forms can provide roots and continuity for Christian education amid all the changes the future may bring. Additional considerations include the seven specific mandates that can foster openness to God's renewing Christian education in the years to come.[32]

Christians are called to partner with God in shaping the future of education. This partnership calls for a commitment to our Triune God, recognizing that the God who is beyond us promises to accompany us. Jesus' parting words are, "And remember, I am with you always, to the end of the age" (Matt. 28:20). This promise extends to the new age to come in our future. God is beyond us, and we entrust our future to divine hands while being faithful in our teaching ministries.

The essential teaching of this final chapter is the following: God *beyond* us beckons us to embrace the future of Christian education with a living hope. This hope is described in 1 Peter 1:3–9 as one that is not only living (v. 3) but also enduring (v. 4), sustaining (v. 5), and rejoicing (vv. 6–9) in light of God's provision for the future:

> Blessed be the God and Father of our Lord Jesus Christ! By his great mercy he has given us a new birth into a living hope through the resurrection of Jesus Christ from the dead, and into an inheritance that is imperishable, undefiled, and unfading, kept in heaven for you, who are being protected by the power of God through faith for a salvation ready to be revealed in the last time. In this you rejoice, even if now for a little while you have had to suffer various trials, so that the genuineness of your faith—being more precious than gold that, though perishable, is tested by fire—may be found to result in praise and glory and honor when Jesus Christ is revealed. Although you have not seen him, you love him; and even though you do not see him now, you believe in him and rejoice with an indescribable and glorious joy, for you are receiving the outcome of your faith, the salvation of your souls.

I better understood the meaning of this passage on a recent visit to China when I was able to observe how God has blessed Chinese Christians with a living hope. Christian hope sustained them through the difficult years of the Cultural Revolution and the much less traumatic Y2K transition that received global attention. It was my privilege to preach on this passage at the Community Church in Shanghai that had been closed during the Cultural Revolution but now was filled to capacity on a bright Sunday morning, reminding us of the hope of resurrection.

CONCLUSION

God Our Teacher has explored the connections between theology and Christian education. Essential theological teachings are named at the close of each of the six chapters and also in the introduction to this work. A fitting summary is to recount these seven teachings in the order they appear:

1. God is our teacher for this time and all times to come.
2. The Triune God being *for* us is the essential starting point for understanding the theological foundation of Christian education.
3. God works *despite* us to transform the sin that besets humanity with the offer of salvation that we teach.
4. God *with* us in the person and work of Jesus Christ provides a model for teaching that transcends the millennia.
5. God *in* us assures us of an empowered partnership for teaching through the person and work of the Holy Spirit.
6. God works *through* us in the teaching ministries of the church that extend God's mission in the world.
7. God *beyond* beckons us to embrace the future of Christian education with a living hope.

Having named these theological essentials, the greater task for Christian teachers is to firmly build our teaching practice on them. Jesus captured the essence of that task in his words recorded in Matthew 7:24–29:

"Everyone then who hears these words of mine and acts on them will be like a wise man who built his house on rock. The rain fell, the floods came, and the winds blew and beat on that house, but it did not fall, because it had been founded on rock. And everyone who hears these words of mine and does not act on them will be like a foolish man who built his house on sand. The rain fell, and the floods came, and the winds blew and beat against that house, and it fell—and great was its fall!"

Now when Jesus had finished saying these things, the crowds were astounded at his teaching, for he taught them as one having authority, and not as their scribes.

Theological basics provide the bedrock on which to build Christian education. The choice is ours in the theory and practice of Christian education, whether to build upon these essentials or to opt for the shifting sands of educational fads in the wider culture. I do not equate my words and thoughts in this work as the only rock on which to build. That would be assuming the arrogance of a foolish man. Rather, I offer this work with the prayer that Jesus' words and exemplary model for Christian education might be discovered by those who follow after him in their teaching.

CROSSING OVER TO POSTMODERNITY: EDUCATIONAL INVITATIONS

Crossing over is an experience affirmed in biblical accounts. Crossing over is central to our calling as pilgrims or sojourners in faith. The anticipation of crossing over is fraught with a sense of adventure, awe, and apprehension. Nevertheless, the experience of moving from one locale or realm to another invites the possibility of transformation that is central to the journey of faith with our Triune God. God is in the business of bringing new life and sustaining life beyond what humans conceive is feasible or desirable. The cultural shift to postmodernity provides an occasion for transformation that God will bring to persons, families, communities, churches, societies, structures, and creation itself. The occasion of a cultural shift does not assume faithfulness to God's purposes or intentions. Spiritual discernment is required to affirm those changes God intends and oppose those that distort God's will for humanity and all of creation.

In May 2000, I traveled along with eighteen other delegates from Andover Newton Theological School to Mainland China. This was the first opportunity I had to cross over the Pacific Ocean to visit Chinese churches and seminaries. I witnessed the spiritual vitality of Christians who suffered much during the Cultural Revolution. My sense of hope was renewed in seeing how God has sustained their faith, honoring their prayers and the prayers of other Christians across the globe. The fervent commitment of Chinese Christians to mission in a rapidly changing society encouraged all members of our delegation. Crossing over to China with open hearts and minds provided fertile ground for God's Spirit to work and foster vision. This contemporary experience of crossing over parallels what the Bible describes in both the Old and New Testaments.

Old Testament Crossings

The most dramatic accounts of crossing over describe how the nation of Israel was both formed and transformed at critical points in its history. The classic film *The Ten Commandments* portrays the dramatic crossing of the Red Sea (Exod. 14) in Hollywood fashion. In that crossing from Egypt to Sinai, an infant nation was delivered by God's mighty hand. A diverse or mixed crowd of people departed from Egypt (Exod. 12:38), and their liberation came at great cost to their oppressors. But every stranger or alien had access to the spiritual blessings of the new covenant forged with God provided they fulfilled its obligations (Exod. 12:48).[1] A second crossing is recorded in the crossing of the Jordan River (Josh. 1–4). The first crossing, though dramatic, did not lead to full liberation but a forty-year wilderness trek. A second crossing was required to enter the Promised Land on the terms God intended. Even Moses, the nation's leader, was ineligible for this second crossing and had to step aside for new leadership to emerge in the person of Joshua.

New crossings may well require younger leadership to step up during a time of significant transition in faith communities. This shift can be seen more dramatically in the case of Elijah and Elisha with their personal crossings of the Jordan. Second Kings 2:1–14 recounts how Elisha crossed over the Jordan River and was empowered to address new challenges of prophetic ministry following the crossing of Elijah to heaven in a whirlwind. The transference of leadership was symbolized by Elisha receiving Elijah's mantle. Elisha persisted in pursuing Elijah across the river and requested to receive the firstborn's inherited portion of spirit and power. In the stories of Moses and Elijah, who stand as anchors for Israel's faithful leadership, crossings loom as central to address national and personal challenges.

New Testament Crossings

In the New Testament, the person and ministry of Jesus are preeminent. Jesus crosses over from his preincarnate state to his humanity in a profoundly simple and dramatic fashion, reversing Elijah's departure. He comes as an infant born in the most humble of settings and under difficult circumstances that included Roman domination of the nation Israel. In the multicultural setting of Galilee, he crosses over many barriers to include Gentiles, women, and children in his teaching. He also crosses over from the multicultural backwater of Galilee to Judea and Jerusalem in outrageously proclaiming the kingdom of God in his person. In addition to Jesus' public crossings, in his teaching through parables he honors the more personal crossing of the Good Samaritan in Luke 10:25–37. In this story, the Samaritan travelling on the road from Jerusalem to Jericho crosses over to minister to the injured Jewish merchant. Jesus recognizes the Samaritan as being what Paul describes as a true Jew of the heart (Rom. 2:28–29).

Crossing Over to Postmodernity

Commentators on popular culture and philosophical trends note that we are in the process of crossing over to postmodernity. In this cultural shift, God invites those of us who teach to cross over in heart, mind, spirit, and body. God delights to use those who are willing to cross over, and we must ask ourselves whether this particular crossing brings us to a wilderness, a Promised Land, or some combination of both. Jesus, the author and finisher of our Christian faith, was willing to cross over in his incarnation and earthly ministry. Jesus serves as the model for teaching. Can Christian teachers do less?

My study of the theological foundations for Christian education has celebrated the Trinity as the main taproot. The life revealed in the Trinity and offered to humanity satisfies the deep spiritual hunger of postmodern persons. Sharing the Christian faith with postmodern persons by speaking to their context with sustaining and sustainable content is the challenge facing Christian educators.

The realities of postmodernity find expression in the rising influence of Generation X and the call to reevaluate Christian teaching in relation to their participation. My earlier work on postmodernity in *Foundational Issues in Christian Education* stresses the place of truth that is appropriately questioned within postmodernity.[2] The necessary complement to that discussion considers the place of love or care in Christian education. This follows from the scriptural principle in education of "speaking the truth in love" (Eph. 4:15), which includes actions as well as words.[3] To speak the truth in love in a postmodern context requires attention to the deep hunger for genuine relationships and community being voiced by members of Generation X.[4] Christians claim that the ultimate fulfillment of that hunger can be found in experiencing the love of God and the care of the Christian community. For that to be the case, Christians engaged in education will need to consider the following seven invitations in their educational thought and practice:[5]

1. Return to relational bonds revealed in the Trinity
2. Revisit the communal commitments that shape our lives
3. Reaffirm the "common good" in the societal and global context, and form a public theology
4. Reconsider the place of conscience in the search for wisdom
5. Reinvest in the prophetic calling in pursuing God's politics in the world
6. Reappropriate the joy of celebration in corporate worship and public festival

7. Recognize the continual demand for renewal, reformation, and revolution that God intends until the consummation

The relevance, order, and embrace of these invitations will vary with the particular context of ministry, but the challenge remains if Christians are to minister effectively in postmodern settings.

The return to relational bonds revealed in the Trinity requires Christians to clarify their theological grounding. I affirm that the Trinity can serve as an organizing theological theme for Christian education. This idea is not new, but its application to postmodern realities calls for a return to this Christian distinctive. James Smart, in his classic work *The Teaching Ministry of the Church*, suggested that the doctrine of the Trinity is the essential starting point for understanding the theological bases of Christian education.[6] Nels Ferré, a systematic theologian who worked with renowned Christian educator D. Campbell Wyckoff, proposed a trinitarian model with God the Father as the educator, Jesus Christ the Son as the exemplar, and the Holy Spirit as the tutor.[7] Christian education strives to enable students to explore the mystery and wonder of the Trinity and to taste the community life modeled for humanity in the life of the Trinity. This monumental task calls for the reflection, commitment, and hard work of Christian educators.

Trinitarian grammar also applies to the general tasks of education suggested by the work of Peter Hodgson in *God's Wisdom*. Hodgson, for example, proposes three basic elements for higher education that include critical thinking, heightened imagination, and liberating practice.[8] These relate to my educational trinity in that critical thinking parallels *content*, heightened imagination parallels *persons'* creativity, and liberating practice parallels the *context* of the community and society. I define education as the process of sharing *content* with *persons* in the *context* of their community and society. God the Father as creator is the educator from whom all the *content* of education issues. God's wisdom is what distinguishes education that results in transformation. Jesus the Son as mentor is the model who exemplifies all that a teacher should be in his relationships with other *persons.* The hunger for love and care finds fulfillment in the person of Jesus and all who follow him in their teaching ministries. The Holy Spirit as tutor is the counselor or community consultant who sustains the life of the Christian community and wider society in ways that fulfill God's purposes for the *context.* The Holy Spirit encounters human spirits to bring new life on personal, communal, societal, and global levels. Spiritual renewal applies to the public levels of life as well as the personal and private domains. In relation to theological education, Hodgson's basic elements can be renamed to include theological reflection, spiritual imagination, and transformative practice that fulfill the Triune God's purposes and politics in this world.

In the light of the life revealed for humanity by the Trinity, Christians are called to revisit the communal commitments that shape our lives. Postmodernity shatters the myth of the autonomous individual totally divorced from the bonds of tradition, family, and community. Postmodernity also shatters the claim for objective reason divorced from the place of human interests and existential concerns. The use of language itself represents communal practices and nuances. Persons as viewing subjects and their history affect the terms and directions of their communication. Knowledge itself is recognized as a social construction, and the veracity of various input from media like the Internet must be questioned. Public disclosures are subject to "spin doctors" who provide a host of interpretations in making connections with the recipients or viewers of the message. The variety of contacts and inputs in postmodern life require careful discernment to sort out the barrage of information packaged and disseminated. In order to sift wisdom from the vast amount of knowledge with its claims for immediate attention, Christians must discern the nature and extent of their commitments to various human associations.

Educators have explored the variety of influences by considering the educational configurations or the educational ecology of persons. An educational configuration is a cluster or network of agencies that pass on a culture or educational content to persons. This concept was fully developed in the pioneering work of educational historian Lawrence Cremin.[9] From the work of Bernard Bailyn, Cremin identified four educational agencies or axes in the colonial U.S. (1607–1783): home, church, community, and economy.[10] In the national period (1783–1876), additional educational agencies and institutions that emerged included schools and a host of voluntary associations such as libraries, museums, and child advocacy groups like the YMCA and YWCA. During the metropolitan period (1876-2000), the rise of the body politic and the media is noteworthy. The relationships and interactions of these various agencies or institutions represent an educational configuration. Cremin's shorthand for describing these relationships is that agencies confirm, complement, and/or contradict each other and have varied impacts on individuals in particular communities dependent upon their distinctive learning styles and histories. Communal commitments can be explored by assessing educational configurations and considering the varying contours over time. Postmodern shifts have resulted in increased contradiction across educational configurations, with a resulting sense of fragmentation. In light of this situation, Christians must clarify their basic commitments as the people of God called to incarnate Christian values in the community and society. In relation to the church and its interaction with other agencies, the educational agenda calls for a response to preserve, redeem, or transform the explicit or implicit curriculum of the corresponding agency. This task requires discernment in weighing alternatives.

While assessing educational configurations, Christians must reaffirm the "common" or public good in the societal and global context. This must be done without losing our Christian identity. Christians affirm the bonds they share with all God's creatures and all of creation. The pursuit of the common good itself is a major task that requires sustained dialogue and a willingness to demonstrate love in the social arena through the pursuit of justice and peace *(shalom)*. The Scriptures describe *shalom* as the fullness of relationship and communion that God intends for all of creation. The identification of the common good for Christians results in educational efforts that affirm both Christian identity and openness to the other.[11] The affirmation of identity preserves Christian distinctives, including the recognition that God has created all persons with intrinsic dignity and worth. The affirmation of openness signals the need to respect and care for all others in educational encounters and, more generally, in life. The extent of the globe's ecological crisis demands attention be given to the common fate that Christians share with humanity and all of created life.

The common good for humanity necessitates occasions to *mix* with non-Christians as well as occasions to *huddle* with persons of like faith in wrestling with past, current, and future challenges around the globe.[12] Truth can be discerned in both the particulars of the Christian faith and insights from other religious and nonreligious sources.[13] By drawing from these various sources in their public discourse, Christians affirm the place of politics, which can be defined as the art of making and keeping persons truly human.[14] Christians share with all humanity the care of creation and the possibility of fullness of life sustained for future generations. This fullness of life Scripture describes as the *shalom* that God intended from creation and will complete at the consummation.

With the identification and reappropriation of the common good comes the need to reconsider the place of conscience in the search for wisdom. Barry Harvey draws upon the work of Paul Lehmann in proposing that Christians focus upon conscience as an organizing principle for their shared life and education.

According to Lehmann, it is only as human motivation and human judgment actually converge within conscience that God and humans "have directly and insistently to do with one another [as] the aims and the direction, the motivations and the decisions, the instruments and the structures of human interrelatedness are forged into a pattern of response—a style of life."[15]

The conscience as the seat of the will requires attention to God's demands from a Christian understanding. God's demands include responsible living in the created world as social, political, economic, intellectual, aesthetic, cultural, and spiritual beings in relationship. As relational beings, persons are accountable to God, others, and themselves. The conscience is that dimension of persons where matters of value, virtue, and character take shape. The Christian community is the context for the formation of Christian conscience.

With the increased fragmentation of the human community and educational configurations, the appeal in public discussions of education is to attend to matters of character formation. As violence and abuse increase in communities viewed as safe havens from urban decline and minority intrusion, the concern in the United States intensifies. The expectation that primary, secondary, and higher education alone can bridge the gaps in both public and private morality must be questioned. Conscience and character formation require strategies that influence all the agencies and institutions of any educational configuration. In light of the increased sense of societal and educational crisis, the question of Christian vocation must be posed. With the persistent interest in transformative education, Christians can share the source of transformation they have in their faith.

As Christians engage their mission in the educational world, they can reinvest in their prophetic calling. The prophetic calling involves pursuing God's politics in the world. What are God's politics, and how do they relate to education? In one sense, education is slow-fuse politics that seeks change in the human situation. The transformation is not directly sought through the legislative, executive, or judicial processes of political and civic bodies. Rather, the audacious claim is that education can transform persons and life through study, dialogue, interaction, research, and expression with others in formal, nonformal, and informal arrangements. The sharing of educational content includes the interface of cognitive, affective, intentional, and behavioral components as the whole being takes on new shape.

The prophetic calling involves posing questions, creating reflective space, and wrestling with alternatives for current arrangements. A necessary prior task is the identification of the current arrangement and its precedents. The commonly identified sequence of learning in a prophetic mode is *to see, to judge*, and *to act*. It must be noted that to act also requires seeing the results of actions. Seeing the results of actions thereby continues the cycle and calls for judgment in evaluation. The sequence presumes certain realities. First, it presumes the prior ability to see, which itself may require learning, although seeing can imply various modalities. Second, it presumes evaluating and understanding categories for judgment and a basis for comparison.

Third, in the case of action, it presumes the empowerment of persons with the voice, choice, and means to act effectively. The hope in prophetic teaching is to equip persons to be all that God intends for them as subjects of divine love and care. God's care implies that Christians must care enough to confront realities that oppress persons and limit the fulfillment of God's *shalom* in all of creation. From a Christian perspective, this is only possible through the person and work of the Holy Spirit in partnership with persons. Reinvestment in the prophetic calling is often associated with struggle in the recovery of hope. Augustine once commented that "hope has two lovely daughters, anger and courage. Anger at the way things are, and courage to see that they need not remain as they are."[16] The complement to the anger and courage of hope is the experience of joy that is so crucial to teaching and life.

Christians engaged in education are called to reappropriate the joy of celebration in public worship and festival. Gabriel Fackre helpfully distinguishes the inreach and the outreach of the church in relation to the task and spiritual gift of *leitourgia* or celebration. The inreach of celebration finds expression through the ministries of corporate worship. The outreach of celebration finds expression in festival.[17] Outreach in public festival serves as an extension of Christian mission in the world. Both worship and festival are vehicles for sharing joy as the complement to anger and courage in the embodiment of hope. In my evangelical opinion, joy is the emotion closest to the heart of God. The gospel denotes good news that leads to the experience and expression of joy, even in the midst of loss and suffering. Joy finds its fullest expression in the shared human experiences of worship. In a different mode, this joy is also experienced in occasions of public festival where the gifts of human life and community are celebrated.

The expression of joy in worship and festival are forms of nonformal and informal education in which life is viewed from the perspective of God's heart. The conscience is engaged in worship. But as Archbishop William Temple once described, there is so much more to it: "To worship is to quicken the conscience by the holiness of God, to feed the mind with the truth of God, to purge the imagination by the beauty of God, to open the heart to the love of God, to devote the will to the purpose of God."[18] Worship of this kind is both formative and transformative. In festival, the gift of human life and the beauty of creation are celebrated. Opportunities for creative expression in the arts and music can give glory to God as they are shared in public settings. Recounting the history and recognizing the cultures of various communities can glorify the creator of all culture and history. The postmodern world hungers for the genuine experience of joy that Christians can share through worship and festival.

The seventh invitation of postmodernity is to recognize the continual demand of renewal, reformation, and revolution that God intends until the consummation. Given the nature of created life reflected in the changing seasons of the natural and human life span, openness to transformation is required. New life springs forth in a variety of ways, and rising generations inevitably see the world with different eyes, postmodern eyes. Christian sources describe the need for a continuous process of being reformed, transformed, and renewed by the gracious ministry of the Holy Spirit. In relation to education, this implies a reforming, transforming, and liberating approach.[19]

In any Christian education effort, evaluation is a crucial element that invites the possibility of change in future efforts.[20] Evaluation can also signal the need for openness to the work of the Holy Spirit in recognizing the limits of human efforts. The danger in all education is an idolatry that baptizes the content, methods, forms, or relationships as divine equivalents. Any of these vehicles can be graciously used to accomplish God's purposes. Nevertheless, they all fall short of God's ideals as modeled in the life and ministry of Jesus the Christ. The inevitable gaps serve as an incentive to rely prayerfully on God's resources in the person and ministry of the Holy Spirit and the critical role of the Scriptures. Such reliance welcomes the place of renewal, reformation, and, on occasion, revolution in Christian education. The Spirit brings new life as Christians spiritually discern alternatives to existing patterns and rely on the Spirit's transformation. The Scriptures present new vistas and reveal us and our educational efforts from the perspective of perennial and enduring forms and principles grounded in our Triune God.

Postmodernity provides an occasion for reflection and reconsideration of educational theory and practice.

Conclusion

This appendix has identified seven potential educational invitations of postmodernity for Christian educators. These invitations encourage theological reflection, spiritual imagination, and transformative practice in Christian education that go beyond our current efforts. Discernment is required along with openness to the one seated on the throne who declares, "See, I am making all things new" (Rev. 21:5).

NOTES

Introduction

1. Peter C. Hodgson, *God's Wisdom: Toward a Theology of Education* (Louisville: Westminster/John Knox, 1999). Hodgson does not propose a theology of or for Christian education, but rather a Christian theology of general education (p. 123). His work is provocative and insightful as a complement to this work. On the wisdom theme, also see Charles F. Melchert, *Wise Teaching: Biblical Wisdom and Educational Ministry* (Harrisburg, Pa.: Trinity, 1998).

2. For a systematic theologian's thoughts on the connections between theology and Christian education, see Gabriel Fackre, "The Theological Commonplaces of Christian Education," *Christian Education Journal* 15 (spring 1995): 27–36.

3. Robert W. Pazmiño, *Principles and Practices of Christian Education: An Evangelical Perspective* (Grand Rapids: Baker, 1992), 10–11.

4. Samuel Solivan, *The Spirit, Pathos and Liberation: Toward an Hispanic Pentecostal Theology* (Sheffield: Sheffield Academic Press, 1998), 60–69.

5. Bernard Ramm, *An Evangelical Christology* (Nashville: Thomas Nelson, 1985), 77–79, as cited in Solivan, *The Spirit, Pathos and Liberation,* 81.

6. For an in-depth discussion of the plenitude of God's grace in relation to the Trinity and religious plurality, see the work of my colleague S. Mark Heim, *The Depth of the Riches: A Trinitarian Theology of Religious Ends* (Grand Rapids: Eerdmans, 2000), 123–296.

Chapter 1: God For Us

1. James D. Smart, *The Teaching Ministry of the Church: An Examination of the Basic Principles of Christian Education* (Philadelphia: Westminster, 1954), 10.

2. See my discussion of the postmodern challenge of proclaiming truth in Robert W. Pazmiño, *Foundational Issues in Christian Education: An Introduction in Evangelical Perspective,* 2d ed. (Grand Rapids: Baker, 1997), 243–51.

3. See my chapter, "Surviving or Thriving in the Third Millennium?" and those of other contributors in *Forging a Better Religious Education in the Third Millenium,* ed. James M. Lee (Birmingham, Ala.: Religious Education Press, 2000), 69–88.

4. Nels F. S. Ferré, *A Theology of Christian Education* (Philadelphia: Westminster, 1967). See my earlier discussion of this work in Robert W. Pazmiño, *By What Authority Do We Teach? Sources for Empowering Christian Educators* (Grand Rapids: Baker, 1994), 20–29.

5. Karl Barth, *Evangelical Theology,* trans. Grover Foley (Garden City, N.Y.: Doubleday, 1964), 161.

6. Peter Toon, *Our Triune God: A Biblical Portrayal of the Trinity* (Wheaton: Victor, 1996).

7. Abraham Joshua Heschel, *I Asked for Wonder: A Spiritual Anthology,* ed. Samuel H. Dresner (New York: Crossroad, 1995), 83.

8. Howard E. Butt, Jr., *Renewing America's Soul: A Spiritual Psychology for Home, Work, and Nation* (New York: Continuum, 1996).

9. Ibid., 201, 217.

10. Catherine Mowry LaCugna, *God for Us: The Trinity and Christian Life* (San Francisco: Harper, 1973). For a helpful discussion of LaCugna's work, see Millard J. Erickson, *God in Three Persons: A Contemporary Interpretation of the Trinity* (Grand Rapids: Baker, 1995).

11. Ibid., 1.

12. I differ from LaCugna in not limiting God's revelation to soteriology and reserving a place for ontology that vastly distinguishes human and divine realities. I affirm her effort to relate trinitarian understandings to Christian life and practice. See Erickson, *God in Three Persons,* 307–9.

13. See Robert W. Pazmiño, *Principles and Practices of Christian Education: An Evangelical Perspective* (Grand Rapids: Baker, 1992).

14. Richard R. Osmer, "A New Clue for Religious Education?" in *Forging a Better Religious Education in the Third Millennium,* ed. James M. Lee (Birmingham, Ala.: Religious Education Press, 2000), 196.

15. As cited by John N. Mulder, "Conversion," in *Harper's Encyclopedia of Religious Education,* ed. Iris V. Cully and Kendig B. Cully (San Francisco: Harper and Row, 1990), 163.

16. Barth, *Evangelical Theology,* 8. For Barth, the God of Schleiermacher stresses God's immanence to the exclusion of God's otherness and transcendence. For Barth, God is wholly other and stands in judgment of human sin. God offers mercy in Jesus Christ to remedy the radical plight of human sin that God alone can address.

17. Leonardo Boff, *Trinity and Society: Theology and Liberation* (Maryknoll, N.Y.: Orbis, 1988), 89.

18. See Carol Lakey Hess, *Caretakers of Our Common House: Women's Development in Communities of Faith* (Nashville: Abingdon, 1997), 38. She points out that pride is not always a sin and self-sacrifice sometimes is because "self development

is a higher duty than self-sacrifice." From this work we can affirm that we need to be caretakers of our own house (ourselves) as well as our common house (faith community).

19. Gabriel Fackre, "The Theological Commonplaces of Christian Education," *Christian Education Journal* 15 (spring 1995): 30.

20. Barth, *Evangelical Theology*, 23.

21. Toon, *Our Triune God*, 83.

22. Ibid.; Toon cites Augustine, *On the Holy Trinity*, vol. 3 of A Select Library of Nicene and Post Nicene Fathers (Grand Rapids: Eerdmans, 1956), 47 n. 3.

23. Toon, *Our Triune God*, 83.

24. Ibid., 84.

25. Ibid.

26. Ibid.

27. Robert W. Pazmiño, *Basics of Teaching for Christians: Preparation, Instruction, and Evaluation* (Grand Rapids: Baker, 1998), 11–12.

28. Walter Brueggemann, *Genesis: A Bible Commentary for Teaching and Preaching* (Atlanta: John Knox, 1982), 158–61.

29. Barth, *Evangelical Theology*, 182.

30. For a fuller discussion of the problem of reductionism, see Pazmiño, *Principles and Practices*, 158–61.

31. I discuss the five values of truth, love, faith, hope, and joy in Pazmiño, *Basics of Teaching*, 76–98.

32. Barth, *Evangelical Theology*, 81.

33. William Temple, *The Hope of a New World* (London: SCM, 1941), 30.

34. Max L. Stackhouse, *Public Theology and Political Economy* (Grand Rapids: Eerdmans, 1980), 32–34.

35. Pazmiño, *Principles and Practices*, 10–11, 23–24.

36. For a discussion of the dangers of reductionism, see ibid., 157–63.

37. Pazmiño, *Basics of Teaching*, 21, 26, 67.

38. See my discussion of issues of authority and power in Pazmiño, *By What Authority?*

39. D. Campbell Wyckoff identified these questions in *Theory and Design of Christian Education Curriculum* (Philadelphia: Westminster, 1961), and more recently Thomas Groome uses these in *Christian Religious Education: Sharing Our Story and Vision* (San Francisco: Harper and Row, 1980), xiv. The additional question that Wyckoff named is what organizing principle holds it all together? This chapter proposes that the theological principle of the Trinity can serve as that organizing principle.

40. D. Campbell Wyckoff, Albuquerque, N.Mex., letter to Robert Pazmiño, Newton Centre, Mass., 20 September 1997.

41. I develop this analysis drawing upon the work of Nels Ferré in Pazmiño, *By What Authority?* 20–36.

42. Eldin Villafañe, *The Liberating Spirit: Toward an Hispanic American Pentecostal Social Ethic* (Grand Rapids: Eerdmans, 1993). Also see Eldin Villafañe, *Seek the Peace of the City: Reflections on Urban Ministry* (Grand Rapids: Eerdmans, 1995).

43. Susanne Johnson, *Christian Spiritual Formation in the Church and Classroom* (Nashville: Abingdon, 1989), 143–46.

44. Marianne Sawicki, *The Gospel in History: Portrait of a Teaching Church: The Origins of Christian Education* (New York: Paulist, 1988), 35–36.

45. Lois LeBar, *Children in the Bible School* (Westwood, N.J.: Revell, 1952), 193–94.

46. Julie Gorman, quoted in a promotional pamphlet for Pazmiño, *Basics of Teaching*.

47. Pazmiño, *Basics of Teaching*, 9.

48. See James M. Lee, *The Shape of Religious Instruction: A Social Science Approach* (Birmingham, Ala.: Religious Education Press, 1971); James M. Lee, *The Flow of Religious Instruction* (Birmingham, Ala.: Religious Education Press, 1973); and James M. Lee, *The Content of Religious Instruction: A Social Science Approach* (Birmingham, Ala.: Religious Education Press, 1985).

49. Peter C. Hodgson, *God's Wisdom: Toward a Theology of Education* (Louisville: Westminster/John Knox, 1999), 8, 114–24. The other scholars he names are Rebecca Chopp, who identifies three forms of knowing appropriate for theological education as justice, dialogue, and imagination in *Saving Work: Feminist Practices of Theological Education* (Louisville: Westminster/John Knox, 1995), chap. 5; and Martha Nussbaum, who identifies three capacities essential to the cultivation of humanity today: critical examination of oneself and one's tradition, ability to see beyond oneself to all other human beings by ties of recognition and concern, and narrative imagination, in her work *Cultivating Humanity: A Classical Defense of Reform in Liberal Education* (Cambridge: Harvard University Press, 1997), 9–10.

50. Margaret Ann Crain, "Listening to Churches: Christian Education in Congregational Life," in *Mapping Christian Education: Approaches to Congregational Learning*, ed. Jack L. Seymour (Nashville: Abingdon, 1997), 105–6.

51. Barth, *Evangelical Theology*, 152. Richard R. Osmer explores the qualification of a "teachable spirit" in *A Teachable Spirit: Recovering the Teaching Office in the Church* (Louisville: Westminster/John Knox, 1990).

52. D. Campbell Wyckoff identifies the need in educational thought for an organizing principle that serves to hold things all together in *Theory and Design of Christian Education Curriculum*.

53. For a discussion of a theological anthropology in relation to the psychological foundations of Christian education, see Pazmiño, *Foundational Issues*, 192–93, 217–22.

54. Martin Buber, "The Education of Character," in *Between Man and Man*, trans. Donald Gregor Smith (Boston: Beacon, 1955), 116–17, as cited in Hodgson, *God's Wisdom*, 4.

Chapter 2: God Despite Us

1. Karl Menninger, *Whatever Became of Sin?* (New York: Hawthorn, 1973).

2. See my discussion of amoral development in Robert W. Pazmiño, *Foundational Issues in Christian Education*, 2d ed. (Grand Rapids: Baker, 1997), 205–8.

3. Perry G. Downs, *Teaching for Spiritual Growth: An Introduction to Christian Education* (Grand Rapids: Zondervan, 1994), 54–55.

4. Ronald Habermas and Klaus Issler, *Teaching for Reconciliation: Foundations and Practice of Christian Educational Ministry* (Grand Rapids: Baker, 1992), 50.

5. Downs, *Teaching for Spiritual Growth*, 50.

6. See James E. Loder, *The Logic of the Spirit: Human Development in Theological Perspective* (San Francisco: Jossey-Bass, 1998) to explore the spiritual dynamics in human development.

7. Nicholas Wolterstorff, *Educating for Responsible Action* (Grand Rapids: Eerdmans, 1980), 109.

8. See my discussion of these stages in Robert W. Pazmiño, *Basics of Teaching for Christians: Preparation, Instruction, and Evaluation* (Grand Rapids: Baker, 1998).

9. I recount the exilic model of teaching in Robert W. Pazmiño, *Latin American Journey: Insights for Christian Education in North America* (Cleveland: United Church Press, 1994), 123–46.

10. For an introduction to the Christian story, see Gabriel Fackre and Dorothy Fackre, *Christian Basics: A Primer for Pilgrims* (Grand Rapids: Eerdmans, 1991).

11. Ibid., 19–22.

12. Ibid., 20–21.

13. Ibid., 21–22.

14. See Lawrence O. Richards, *Creative Bible Teaching* (Chicago: Moody, 1970), 112–13; and La Verne Tolbert, *Teaching Like Jesus: A Practical Guide to Christian Education in Your Church* (Grand Rapids: Zondervan, 2000), 108–9.

15. My use of "cook" is in keeping with the dominant metaphor I propose for teaching as "artfully setting an inviting table that welcomes all to participate and results in joyful celebration." See Pazmiño, *Basics of Teaching*, 11.

16. See Loder, *The Logic of the Spirit.*

17. Augustine of Hippo, *Confessions* (Grand Rapids: Sovereign Grace, 1971), 1.

18. Downs, *Teaching for Spiritual Growth*, 54.

19. See Pazmiño, *Basics of Teaching* for a description of these three phases of teaching and the teachers' partnership with God in the effort.

20. Gabriel Fackre, "The Theological Commonplaces of Christian Education," *Christian Education Journal* 15 (spring 1995): 31.

21. Ibid., 34.

22. Ibid.

23. See Habermas and Issler, *Teaching for Reconciliation*, 183, as derived from James W. Fowler, *Becoming Adult, Becoming Christian: Adult Development and Christian Faith* (San Francisco: Harper and Row, 1984), 103–5.

24. John H. Westerhoff, *Spiritual Life: The Foundation for Preaching and Teaching* (Louisville: Westminster/John Knox, 1994), 53–55.

25. Ibid., 55–56.

26. Ibid., 57.

27. Ibid., 58.

28. Ibid., 1.

29. Cited in Tolbert, *Teaching Like Jesus*, 109.

30. Abraham J. Heschel, *Between God and Man: An Interpretation of Judaism from the Writings of Abraham Heschel*, ed. Fritz A. Rothschild (New York: Free Press, 1959), 129–51.

31. For my lessons from Latin America, see Pazmiño, *Latin American Journey*.

32. See Gene A. Getz, *Sharpening the Focus of the Church* (Chicago: Moody, 1974), and also my discussion of Matthew in Pazmiño, *Foundational Issues*, 33–36.

33. For my discussion of the place of liberation theology in relation to education, see Pazmiño, *Latin American Journey*.

34. See Robert W. Pazmiño, *Principles and Practices of Christian Education: An Evangelical Perspective* (Grand Rapids: Baker, 1992), 37–57; and Pazmiño, *Latin American Journey*, 55–75.

Chapter 3: God With Us

1. Portions of this chapter originally appeared as "Jesus: The Master Teacher," in *Introducing Christian Education: Foundations for the Twenty-first Century*, ed. Michael J. Anthony (Grand Rapids: Baker, 2001).

2. See Charles F. Melchert, *Wise Teaching: Biblical Wisdom and Educational Ministry* (Harrisburg, Pa.: Trinity, 1998). In chapter 6 of his work, Melchert addresses the theme, "Why Didn't Jesus Tell Bible Stories?" 205–71.

3. See my discussion of this definition in Robert W. Pazmiño, *Principles and Practices of Christian Education: An Evangelical Perspective* (Grand Rapids: Baker, 1992), 10, 31.

4. Gabriel Moran, *Showing How: The Act of Teaching* (Valley Forge, Pa.: Trinity, 1997), 39.

5. Richard R. Osmer, "A New Clue for Religious Education?" in *Forging a Better Religious Education in the Third Millennium*, ed. James M. Lee (Birmingham, Ala.: Religious Education Press, 2000), 188. Also see James E. Loder, *The Logic of the Spirit: Human Development in Theological Perspective* (San Francisco: Jossey-Bass, 1998), 37–38.

6. Osmer, "A New Clue for Religious Education?" 188.

7. Peter C. Hodgson, *God's Wisdom: Toward a Theology of Education* (Louisville: Westminster/John Knox, 1999), 140.

8. Pazmiño, *Principles and Practices*, 10–11.

9. In exploring this question, also see the most recent work of La Verne Tolbert, *Teaching Like Jesus: A Practical Guide to Christian Education in Your Local Church* (Grand Rapids: Zondervan, 2000).

10. Bernard Bailyn defines education as "the entire process by which a culture transmits itself across the generations." See Bernard Bailyn, *Education in the Forming of American Society: Needs and Opportunities for Study* (New York: Norton, 1960), 14, 45. This definition of education emphasizes the processes of socialization and enculturation in passing on a culture across the generations. Bailyn, in his study of colonial America, identifies four great axes of society that serve to pass on a culture: family, church, community, and economy. Note that Bailyn

does not list schools, although schools are what most people associate with education. A question to consider is why Bailyn does not list them.

11. For an introduction to the rabbinic tradition, see James L. Crenshaw, *Education in Ancient Israel: Across the Deadening Silence* (New York: Doubleday, 1998).

12. Robert H. Stein, *The Method and Message of Jesus' Teachings* (Philadelphia: Westminster, 1978).

13. Two works that explore this relationship between continuity and change are Mary Elizabeth Moore, *Education for Continuity and Change: A New Model for Christian Religious Education* (Nashville: Abingdon, 1983); and Padraic O'Hare, ed., *Tradition and Transformation in Religious Education* (Birmingham, Ala: Religious Education Press, 1979). Also see Mary Boys, *Educating in Faith: Maps and Visions* (San Francisco: Harper and Row, 1989), 193, where Boys defines religious education as "the making accessible of the traditions of the religious community and the making manifest of the intrinsic connection between traditions and transformation."

14. See my discussion of Galilee in Robert W. Pazmiño, *Latin American Journey: Insights for Christian Education in North America* (Cleveland: United Church Press, 1994), 108–10, where I draw upon Kenneth W. Clark, "Galilee," in *Interpreter's Dictionary of the Bible*, ed. George A. Buttrick (Nashville: Abingdon, 1962), 344–47. Also see Virgil Elizondo, *Galilean Journey: The Mexican-American Promise* (Maryknoll, N.Y.: Orbis, 1983) for a theological discussion of Galilee's significance in understanding cultural realities.

15. Orlando Costas describes the legacy of Jesus from the Galilean periphery as providing a guide for mission in *Liberating News: A Theology of Contextual Evangelization* (Grand Rapids: Eerdmans, 1989), 49–70.

16. For my discussion of multicultural Christian education, see Pazmiño, *Latin American Journey*, 106–22. Also see James Breckenridge and Lillian Breckenridge, *What Color Is Your God? Multicultural Education in the Church* (Wheaton: Victor, 1995); and Barbara Wilkerson, ed., *Multicultural Religious Education* (Birmingham, Ala.: Religious Education Press, 1997).

17. Ricardo L. García, *Teaching in a Pluralistic Society: Concepts, Models, Strategies* (New York: Harper and Row, 1982), 8.

18. See Robert W. Pazmiño, *Foundational Issues in Christian Education: An Introduction in Evangelical Perspective*, 2d ed. (Grand Rapids: Baker, 1997), 243–51. This appendix is titled, "Singing the Lord's Song in a Foreign Land: Proclaiming Truth in a Postmodern Setting," and looks to the first-century example of Jesus as suggestive for contemporary challenges to teaching with the questions posed by postmodernism.

19. Herman Horne, *Jesus the Teacher: Examining His Expertise in Education*, revised and updated by Angus M. Gunn (Grand Rapids: Kregel, 1998).

20. Ibid., 135–36.

21. For a study of authority in relation to teaching, see Robert W. Pazmiño, *By What Authority Do We Teach? Sources for Empowering Christian Educators* (Grand Rapids: Baker, 1994). Jesus' authority is discussed on pp. 24–26.

22. James Stewart outlines these areas in *The Life and Teaching of Jesus Christ* (Nashville: Abingdon, 1978), 64–71, which I elaborate upon in Pazmiño, *Principles and Practices*, 125–29.

23. These areas are elaborated in Pazmiño, *Foundational Issues*, 33–36.

24. Roland G. Kuhl, "The Reign of God: Implications for Christian Education," *Christian Education Journal*, n.s., 1 (fall 1997): 73–88.

25. See Pazmiño, *Foundational Issues*, 13–14; and Pazmiño, *Principles and Practices*, 9–10.

26. Pazmiño, *Latin American Journey*, 102–3; but also see 84–88 where I consider both an equilibrium and conflict paradigm.

27. My reluctance to identify one paradigm relates to my identity as a North American Hispanic person who affirms a both/and perspective on life. This perspective maintains that there is "more than one way of looking at things," as theologian Roberto Goizueta suggests. See Eduardo C. Fernández, *La Cosecha: Harvesting Contemporary United States Hispanic Theology (1972–1998)* (Collegeville, Minn.: Liturgical Press, 2000), 54. Fernández suggests that "the good news is that life and theology are much more complex than models" and, I would add, paradigms (157). See my discussion of "Double Dutch" and Galilee in *Latin American Journey*, 106–10.

28. Isaiah Berlin, *The Hedgehog and the Fox* (Chicago: Ivan R. Dee, 1993).

29. One of my students, Katharine Preston, who is a student of nature and an ecological educator, pointed out that Berlin mistypes the hedgehog and might have better used the badger as an example of a hole digger.

30. Robert W. Pazmiño, *Basics of Teaching for Christians: Preparation, Instruction, and Evaluation* (Grand Rapids: Baker, 1998), 76–99.

31. Ibid., 89–94.

32. For a discussion of transformation in relation to teaching, see Jim Wilhoit, *Christian Education and the Search for Meaning*, 2d ed. (Grand Rapids: Baker, 1991), 105–14; and Robert W. Pazmiño, *Latin American Journey*, 55–75.

33. Tradition identified the companion of Cleopas in Luke 24:18 to be Simon, but recent scholarship suggests the possibility of the other disciple being Mary identified in John 19:25 as the wife of Clopas, which is another form of the name Cleopas. Mary, the wife of Clopas, was present at the crucifixion and therefore knew of all that happened in Jerusalem as noted in Luke 24:18ff. Christian tradition has not always honored the ministry of the women who ministered to Jesus throughout his earthly journey and were faithful at the crucifixion as compared with his male disciples, who (except for John) deserted him.

34. See Leona M. English, *Mentoring in Religious Education* (Birmingham, Ala.: Religious Education Press, 1998), 213, where English draws upon Eugene M. Anderson, "Definitions of Mentoring," unpublished manuscript, 1987, quoted in Eugene M. Anderson and Anne L. Shannon, "Toward a Conceptualization of Mentoring," *Journal of Teacher Education* 39, no. 1 (1988): 40. For additional works on mentoring, see Shelly Cunningham, "Who's Mentoring the Mentors? The Discipleship Dimension of Faculty Development in Christian Higher Education," in *Theological Education* 34, no. 2 (spring 1998): 31–49; and Edward C. Sellner, *The Ministry of Spiritual Kinship* (Notre Dame, Ind.: Ave Maria, 1990).

35. Robert E. Kelley, *The Power of Followership: How to Create Leaders People Want to Follow and Followers Who Lead Themselves* (New York: Currency Doubleday, 1992), 57–62.

36. A. B. Bruce, *The Training of the Twelve* (1894; reprint, Grand Rapids: Kregel, 1971). Contemporary readers may find the language and some of Bruce's comments regarding the Jews to be problematic. Reading beyond these limitations, which are present in any work, is recommended.

37. Matt Friedeman, *The Master Plan of Teaching: Understanding and Applying the Teaching Styles of Jesus* (Wheaton: Victor, 1990), 200–202.

38. See Edward P. Blair, "Mary," in *The Interpreter's Dictionary of the Bible*, ed. George A. Buttrick (Nashville: Abingdon, 1962), 288–89.

39. Daniel Aleshire, "Finding Eagles in the Turkeys' Nest: Pastoral Theology and Christian Education," *Review and Expositor* 85 (1988): 704.

40. For a fuller discussion of the *anawim*, see Pazmiño, *By What Authority?* 63–65.

41. Roy B. Zuck, *Teaching as Jesus Taught* (Grand Rapids: Baker, 1995), 11–12.

Chapter 4: God In Us

1. These three phases of teaching are discussed in Robert W. Pazmiño, *Basics of Teaching for Christians: Preparation, Instruction, and Evaluation* (Grand Rapids: Baker, 1998) and will be explored later in this chapter.

2. James E. Loder, *The Logic of the Spirit: Human Development in Theological Perspective* (San Francisco: Jossey-Bass, 1998), 120–22.

3. I discuss this interaction in Robert W. Pazmiño, *Foundational Issues in Christian Education*, 2d ed. (Grand Rapids: Baker, 1997), 217–22. Also see Loder, *The Logic of the Spirit*, for an in-depth discussion of the Spirit's presence and ministry in human development.

4. I discuss the nature of this power and the place of authority in teaching in Robert W. Pazmiño, *By What Authority Do We Teach? Sources for Empowering Christian Educators* (Grand Rapids: Baker, 1994).

5. Millard J. Erickson, *Christian Theology*, 2d ed. (Grand Rapids: Baker, 1998), 882–83.

6. Ibid., 883.

7. Ibid.

8. Ibid., 885. Also see my discussion in Robert W. Pazmiño, *Latin American Journey: Insights for Christian Education in North America* (Cleveland: United Church Press, 1994), 123–44.

9. Erickson, *Christian Theology*, 885.

10. Pazmiño, *By What Authority?* 26–27.

11. Ibid., 27.

12. Ibid., 27–28.

13. See my discussion of this connection between teaching and God's mission in Robert W. Pazmiño, *Principles and Practices of Christian Education* (Grand Rapids: Baker, 1992), 37–57, 93–100; and Pazmiño, *By What Authority?* 37–58.

14. Pazmiño, *By What Authority?* 28.

15. Gabriel Fackre, *The Christian Story: A Narrative Interpretation of Basic Christian Doctrine*, rev. ed. (Grand Rapids: Eerdmans, 1984), 23.

16. See Pazmiño, *By What Authority?* 119–46.

17. Erickson, *Christian Theology*, 888.

18. Ibid.

19. Ibid.

20. For a discussion on the place of conversion, see Robert W. Pazmiño, "A Comprehensive Vision for Conversion in Christian Education," *Religious Education* 87 (winter 1992): 87–101; and Pazmiño, *Latin American Journey*, 55–75.

21. For one recent example of the effort to address the need for a public theology, see Benjamin Valentin, "Going Public: Negotiating the Intersections of a Hispanic/Latino and U.S. Public Theology" (Ph.D. diss., Drew University, 2000). Two works that consider Christian education in relation to the public are Jack Seymour, Robert T. O'Gorman, and Charles R. Foster, *The Church in the Education of the Public: Refocusing the Task of Religious Education* (Nashville: Abingdon, 1984); and Mary C. Boys, ed., *Education for Citizenship and Discipleship* (New York: Pilgrim, 1989).

22. Pazmiño, *By What Authority?* 121.

23. Ibid., 143.

24. Alfred McBride, *A Retreat with Pope John XXIII: Opening the Windows to Wisdom* (Cincinnati: St. Anthony Messenger Press, 1996), 40.

25. Pazmiño, *Foundational Issues*, 38–39.

26. Ibid., 39.

27. John Westerhoff, *Spiritual Life: The Foundation for Preaching and Teaching* (Louisville: Westminster/John Knox, 1994).

28. Ibid., 1.

29. Ibid. Also see my discussion of the commandments as they relate to teaching in *Basics of Teaching*, 21, 26, 67, 84.

30. Justo L. González, *Mañana: Christian Theology from a Hispanic Perspective* (Nashville: Abingdon, 1990), 158.

31. Pazmiño, *By What Authority?* 68.

32. Ibid., 68–71.

33. Loder, *The Logic of the Spirit*, 17.

34. Erickson, *Christian Theology*, 897–98.

35. Julie Gorman as quoted in a promotional pamphlet for Pazmiño, *Basics of Teaching*.

36. Parker J. Palmer, *To Know As We Are Known: A Spirituality of Education* (San Francisco: Harper and Row, 1983), as cited in Pazmiño, *Principles and Practices*, 157–58.

37. Palmer, *To Know As We Are Known*, 6–10.

38. Cited in World Council of Churches, *Spiritual Formation in Theological Education*, 8.

39. Pazmiño, *Basics of Teaching*, 15–46.

40. I attribute this Augustine quote to oral tradition.

41. D. Campbell Wyckoff, *The Task of Christian Education* (Philadelphia: Westminster, 1955), 104.

42. Parker J. Palmer, *The Courage to Teach: Exploring the Inner Landscape of a Teacher's Life* (San Francisco: Jossey-Bass, 1998).

43. As cited in Wilbert J. McKeachie, *Teaching Tips: Strategies, Research, and Theory for College and University Teachers* (Lexington, Mass.: Heath, 1994), 384.

44. Norman DeJong, *Education in the Truth* (Nutley, N.J.: Presbyterian & Reformed, 1974), 61–63.

45. Loder, *Logic of the Spirit*, 142.

46. James E. Loder and W. Jim Neidhardt, *The Knight's Move: The Relational Logic of the Spirit in Theology and Science* (Colorado Springs: Helmers and Howard, 1992), 2.

47. Pazmiño, *Foundational Issues*, 68.

48. Arthur Becker, *Ministry with Older Persons* (Minneapolis: Augsburg, 1986), 196, as cited by Harriet Kerr Swenson, *Visible and Vital: A Handbook for the Aging Congregation* (New York: Paulist, 1994), 108, 129.

49. Pazmiño, *Basics of Teaching*, 75–99.

50. Lois E. LeBar, *Education That Is Christian*, ed. James E. Plueddemann (Wheaton: Victor, 1989), 293–304.

51. Peter C. Hodgson, *God's Wisdom: Toward a Theology of Education* (Louisville: Westminster/John Knox, 1999), 6–7.

Chapter 5: God Through Us

1. These are the themes of chapters 1, 3, and 4 respectively.

2. Millard J. Erickson, *Christian Theology*, 2d ed. (Grand Rapids: Baker, 1998), 1044–51.

3. See Robert W. Pazmiño, *Principles and Practices of Christian Education: An Evangelical Perspective* (Grand Rapids: Baker, 1992), 37–57; and Robert W. Pazmiño, *Latin American Journey: Insights for Christian Education in North America* (Cleveland: United Church Press, 1994), 55–75. The five-task model is also discussed in chapter 6 of this work.

4. Avery Dulles, *Models of the Church*, expanded ed. (Garden City, N.Y.: Doubleday, 1987).

5. Gabriel Fackre, "Christ's Ministry and Ours," in *The Laity in Ministry: The Whole People of God for the Whole World*, ed. George Peck and John S. Hoffman (Valley Forge, Pa.: Judson, 1984), 111–15. This is originally cited in Pazmiño, *Principles and Practices*, 77.

6. Others may propose one of the five tasks as serving as the ligaments of the church's ministry and mission. There is warrant for considering advocacy in our postmodern culture where the validity of the gospel requires expression in public life.

7. Erickson, *Christian Theology*, 1045.

8. For a discussion of the *anawim,* see Robert W. Pazmiño, *By What Authority Do We Teach? Sources for Empowering Christian Educators* (Grand Rapids: Baker, 1994), 63–65.

9. Erickson, *Christian Theology,* 1046.

10. Ibid.

11. Ibid., 1047.

12. Ibid.

13. Ibid.

14. Ibid., 1048.

15. Ibid.

16. Roy B. Zuck, "The Role of the Holy Spirit in Christian Teaching," in *The Christian Educator's Handbook on Teaching,* ed. Kenneth O. Gangel and Howard G. Hendricks (Wheaton: Victor, 1988), 39.

17. For a discussion of Matthew's Gospel, see Robert W. Pazmiño, *Foundational Issues in Christian Education: An Introduction in Evangelical Perspective,* 2d ed. (Grand Rapids: Baker, 1997), 33–36.

18. Erickson, *Christian Theology,* 1049.

19. Orlando E. Costas, "Educación Teológica y Misión," in *Nuevas Alternativas de Educación Teológica,* ed. C. René Padilla (Buenos Aires: Nueva Creación; Grand Rapids: Eerdmans, 1986), 9.

20. Pazmiño, *Latin American Journey,* 9–10.

21. Ibid., 11.

22. Gabriel Fackre, *The Christian Story: A Narrative Interpretation of Basic Christian Doctrine,* rev. ed. (Grand Rapids: Eerdmans, 1984), 71.

23. See Arthur Becker, *Ministry with Older Adults* (Minneapolis: Augsburg, 1986), 196, as cited in Harriet Kerr Swenson, *Visible and Vital: A Handbook for the Aging Congregation* (New York: Paulist, 1994), 108, 129 n. 1.

24. David J. Bosch, *Transforming Mission: Paradigm Shifts in Theology of Mission* (Maryknoll, N.Y.: Orbis, 1991), 47.

25. Ibid., 10.

26. Pazmiño, *By What Authority?* 43–44; and Orlando E. Costas, "The Mission and Nature of the Church," paper presented at Andover Newton Theological School, Newton Centre, Mass., 1986, 11.

27. Guillermo Cook, *The Expectation of the Poor: Latin American Base Ecclesial Communities in Protestant Perspective* (Maryknoll, N.Y.: Orbis, 1985), 238.

28. See Robert W. Pazmiño, *Basics of Teaching for Christians: Preparation, Instruction, and Evaluation* (Grand Rapids: Baker, 1998), 79–80; and Elliot Eisner, *The Educational Imagination: On the Design and Evaluation of School Programs,* 2d ed. (New York: Macmillan, 1985), 87–107.

29. Pazmiño, *Basics of Teaching,* 76–98.

30. Ibid., 83–88. In addition, details of this care are suggested in a discussion of the preparation for teaching, 15–46.

31. Cook, *Expectation of the Poor,* 238.

Chapter 6: God Beyond Us

1. For my earlier thoughts on the future of Christian education following a sabbatical trip to Latin America, see Robert W. Pazmiño, *Latin American Journey: Insights for Christian Education in North America* (Cleveland: United Church Press, 1994), 123–46. In this work I find the ministries of Ezra, Nehemiah, and the Levites suggestive for the tasks of rebuilding Christian education in the future.

2. Millard J. Erickson, *Christian Theology*, 2d ed. (Grand Rapids: Baker, 1998), 1171.

3. Ibid.

4. Dorothy Fackre and Gabriel Fackre, *Christian Basics: A Primer for Pilgrims* (Grand Rapids: Eerdmans, 1991), 126.

5. Ibid., 127.

6. Glenn W. Barker, William L. Lane, and J. Ramsey Michaels, *The New Testament Speaks* (New York: Harper and Row, 1969), 271.

7. For a thorough discussion of the place of reconciliation in Christian education, see Ronald Habermas and Klaus Issler, *Teaching for Reconciliation: Foundations and Practice of Christian Educational Ministry* (Grand Rapids: Baker, 1992).

8. Fackre and Fackre, *Christian Basics*, 134–36.

9. Ibid., 135.

10. Ibid.

11. Ibid., 136.

12. See Robert W. Pazmiño, *Principles and Practices of Christian Education: An Evangelical Perspective* (Grand Rapids: Baker, 1992), 157–63, for a discussion of six potential reductionisms.

13. See a full discussion of preparation for teaching in Robert W. Pazmiño, *Basics of Teaching: Preparation, Instruction, and Evaluation* (Grand Rapids: Baker, 1998), 15–46.

14. On the question of authority in teaching, see Robert W. Pazmiño, *By What Authority Do We Teach? Sources for Empowering Christian Educators* (Grand Rapids: Baker, 1994).

15. A helpful work on a holistic understanding of learning is Thom Schultz and Joani Schultz, *The Dirt on Learning: Groundbreaking Tools to Grow Faith in Your Church* (Loveland, Colo.: Group, 1999), which creatively uses the parable of the sower to explore active learning.

16. Abraham Joshua Heschel, *I Asked for Wonder: A Spiritual Anthology*, ed. Samuel H. Dresner (New York: Crossroad, 1995), 83.

17. Abraham Joshua Heschel, *Between God and Man: An Interpretation of Judaism from the Writings of Abraham Heschel*, ed. Fritz A. Rothschild (New York: Free Press, 1959), 129–51.

18. See Pazmiño, *Principles and Practices*, 37–57, and *Latin American Journey*, 55–75.

19. James Loder, *The Logic of the Spirit: Human Development in Theological Perspective* (San Francisco: Jossey-Bass, 1998), 304.

20. Samuel Solivan, *The Spirit, Pathos and Liberation: Toward an Hispanic Pentecostal Theology* (Sheffield: Sheffield Academic Press, 1998), 47–69.

21. The first four of these issues are discussed in Robert W. Pazmiño, "Surviving or Thriving in the Third Millennium?" in *Forging a Better Religious Education in the Third Millennium*, ed. James M. Lee (Birmingham, Ala.: Religious Education Press, 2000), 70–74, and the fifth issue on time perspective is implied in the discussion following the identification of the four educational issues. These issues emerge from a consideration of the Y2K computer problem that plagued our entry into the third millennium. The focus in this edited work was upon the future of religious education in general, whereas my interest here is upon Christian education in particular.

22. For additional consideration of the connection between the five-task model and teaching, see Pazmiño, *Basics of Teaching*, 76–99.

23. I suggested some particular areas for evaluation in Pazmiño, *Principles and Practices*, 163–67.

24. In Pazmiño, *By What Authority?* 39–45, I explore the relationship between God's mission and the nature of more local and particularized missions.

25. Richard R. Osmer, "A New Clue for Religious Education?" in *Forging a Better Religious Education in the Third Millennium*, ed. James M. Lee (Birmingham, Ala.: Religious Education Press, 2000), 188.

26. See my discussion of multicultural education in Pazmiño, *Latin American Journey*, 106–22.

27. Klaus Issler, "The Spiritual Formation of Jesus: The Significance of the Holy Spirit in Jesus' Life," *Christian Education Journal* 4 (fall 2000): 13–14.

28. Ibid., 24.

29. I recount these in Pazmiño, "Surviving or Thriving in the Third Millennium?" 84–87.

30. See Fackre and Fackre, *Christian Basics*.

31. Pazmiño, "Surviving or Thriving in the Third Millennium?" 87.

32. Ibid., 87–88.

Appendix: Crossing Over to Postmodernity

1. Hywel R. Jones, "Exodus," in *The New Bible Commentary*, rev. ed., ed. D. Guthrie and J. A. Motyer (Grand Rapids: Eerdmans, 1970), 127–28.

2. Robert W. Pazmiño, *Foundational Issues in Christian Education: An Introduction in Evangelical Perspective*, 2d ed. (Grand Rapids: Baker, 1997), 243–51.

3. See my discussion of this principle in Robert W. Pazmiño, *Basics of Teaching for Christians: Preparation, Instruction, and Evaluation* (Grand Rapids: Baker, 1998), 67–68, 75–76, 88, 98–99.

4. For a discussion of this hunger, see Tom Beaudoin, *Virtual Faith: The Irreverent Spiritual Quest of Generation X* (San Francisco: Jossey-Bass, 1998).

5. These invitations can be compared with the mandates or invitations shared with the churches in Revelation 2 and 3 noted in chapter 6.

6. James D. Smart, *The Teaching Ministry of the Church: An Examination of the Basic Principles of Christian Education* (Philadelphia: Westminster, 1954), 10.

7. Nels F. S. Ferré, *A Theology for Christian Education* (Philadelphia: Westminster, 1967). See my discussion of this work in Robert W. Pazmiño, *By What Authority Do We Teach? Sources for Empowering Christian Educators* (Grand Rapids: Baker, 1994), 20–29.

8. Peter C. Hodgson, *God's Wisdom: Toward a Theology of Education* (Louisville: Westminster/John Knox, 1999), 8, 114–24.

9. Lawrence A. Cremin, *Traditions of American Education* (New York: Basic, 1976).

10. Bernard Bailyn, *Education in the Forming of American Society: Needs and Opportunities for Study* (New York: Norton, 1960), 45.

11. Constance Tarasar, "The Minority Problem: Educating for Identity and Openness," in *Religious Pluralism and Religious Education*, ed. Norma Thompson (Birmingham, Ala.: Religious Education Press, 1988), 195–210.

12. I discuss the strategy of "huddle and mix" in Robert W. Pazmiño, "Surviving or Thriving in the Third Millennium?" in *Forging a Better Religious Education in the Third Millennium*, ed. James M. Lee (Birmingham, Ala.: Religious Education Press, 2000), 82–83.

13. I discuss this perspective in Pazmiño, *By What Authority?* 119–46.

14. In the tradition of Aristotle, George W. Webber proposes this definition in *The Congregation in Mission* (New York: Abingdon, 1964), 49. In this definition, Webber draws upon the work of Paul Lehmann, *Ethics in a Christian Context* (New York: Harper and Row, 1963), 74–101.

15. Barry Harvey, *Politics of the Theological: Beyond the Piety and Power of a World Come of Age* (New York: Lang, 1995), 12–13. Harvey quotes from Paul L. Lehmann, *Ethics in a Christian Context*, 288.

16. As cited in Wilbert J. McKeachie, *Teaching Tips: Strategies, Research, and Theory for College and University Teachers*, 9th ed. (Lexington, Mass.: Heath, 1994), 384.

17. Gabriel Fackre, *The Christian Story: A Narrative Interpretation of Basic Christian Doctrine*, rev. ed. (Grand Rapids: Eerdmans, 1984), 71.

18. William Temple, *The Hope of a New World* (London: Student Christian Movement Press, 1941), 30.

19. See my discussion of liberation and transformation in Robert W. Pazmiño, *Latin American Journey: Insights for Christian Education in North America* (Cleveland: United Church Press, 1994), 28–75.

20. See my discussion of evaluation in Pazmiño, *Basics of Teaching*, 75–99.

SELECT BIBLIOGRAPHY

God For Us

Barth, Karl. *Evangelical Theology*. Trans. Grover Foley. Garden City, N.Y.: Doubleday, 1964.

Boff, Leonardo. *Trinity and Society: Theology and Liberation*. Maryknoll, N.Y.: Orbis, 1988.

Erickson, Millard J. *God in Three Persons: A Contemporary Interpretation of the Trinity*. Grand Rapids: Baker, 1995.

Fackre, Gabriel. "The Theological Commonplaces of Christian Education." *Christian Education Journal* 15 (spring 1995): 27–36.

Ferré, Nels F. S. *A Theology of Christian Education*. Philadelphia: Westminster, 1967.

Heim, S. Mark. *The Depth of the Riches: A Trinitarian Theology of Religious Ends*. Grand Rapids: Eerdmans, 2000.

Heschel, Abraham Joshua. *I Asked for Wonder: A Spiritual Anthology*. Ed. Samuel H. Dresner. New York: Crossroad, 1995.

Hess, Carol Lakey. *Caretakers of Our Common House: Women's Development in Communities of Faith*. Nashville: Abingdon, 1997.

Hodgson, Peter C. *God's Wisdom: Toward a Theology of Education*. Louisville: Westminster/John Knox, 1999.

LaCugna, Catherine Mowry. *God for Us: The Trinity and Christian Life*. San Francisco: Harper, 1973.

Lawson, Kevin. *Theology and Christian Education: Dialogue on Theological Foundations and Issues Since 1940: An Annotated Bibliography*. Louisville: North American Professors of Christian Education; Colorado Springs: Cook, 1998.

Miller, Randolph C., ed. *Theologies of Religious Education*. Birmingham, Ala.: Religious Education Press, 1995.

Pazmiño, Robert W. *Foundational Issues in Christian Education: An Introduction in Evangelical Perspective.* 2d ed. Grand Rapids: Baker, 1997.

————. *Principles and Practices of Christian Education: An Evangelical Perspective.* Grand Rapids: Baker, 1992.

Seymour, Jack L., and Donald E. Miller, eds. *Theological Approaches to Christian Education.* Nashville: Abingdon, 1990.

Smart, James D. *The Teaching Ministry of the Church: An Examination of the Basic Principles of Christian Education.* Philadelphia: Westminster, 1954.

Solivan, Samuel. *The Spirit, Pathos and Liberation: Toward an Hispanic Pentecostal Theology.* Sheffield: Sheffield Academic Press, 1998.

Stackhouse, Max L. *Public Theology and Political Economy.* Grand Rapids: Eerdmans, 1980.

Thompson, Norma, ed. *Religious Education and Theology.* Birmingham, Ala.: Religious Education Press, 1982.

Toon, Peter. *Our Triune God: A Biblical Portrayal of the Trinity.* Wheaton: Victor, 1996.

God Despite Us

Downs, Perry G. *Teaching for Spiritual Growth: An Introduction to Christian Education.* Grand Rapids: Zondervan, 1994.

Fackre, Dorothy, and Gabriel Fackre. *Christian Basics: A Primer for Pilgrims.* Grand Rapids: Eerdmans, 1991.

Habermas, Ronald, and Klaus Issler. *Teaching for Reconciliation: Foundations and Practice of Christian Education Ministry.* Grand Rapids: Baker, 1992.

Loder, James E. *The Logic of the Spirit: Human Development in Theological Perspective.* San Francisco: Jossey-Bass, 1998.

Menninger, Karl. *Whatever Became of Sin?* New York: Hawthorn, 1973.

Pazmiño, Robert W. *Latin American Journey: Insights for Christian Education in North America.* Cleveland: United Church Press, 1994.

Tolbert, La Verne. *Teaching Like Jesus: A Practical Guide to Christian Education in Your Church.* Grand Rapids: Zondervan, 2000.

Westerhoff, John. *Spiritual Life: The Foundation for Preaching and Teaching.* Louisville: Westminster/John Knox, 1994.

Wolterstorff, Nicholas. *Educating for Responsible Action.* Grand Rapids: Eerdmans, 1980.

God With Us

Bruce, A. B. *The Training of the Twelve*. 1894. Reprint, Grand Rapids: Kregel, 1971.

Crenshaw, James L. *Education in Ancient Israel: Across the Deadening Silence*. New York: Doubleday, 1998.

Elizondo, Virgil. *Galilean Journey: The Mexican-American Promise*. Maryknoll, N.Y.: Orbis, 1983.

English, Leona M. *Mentoring in Religious Education*. Birmingham, Ala.: Religious Education Press, 1998.

Friedeman, Matt. *The Master Plan of Teaching: Understanding and Applying the Teaching Styles of Jesus*. Wheaton: Victor, 1990.

Horne, Herman. *Jesus the Teacher: Examining His Expertise in Education*. Revised and updated by Angus M. Gunn. Grand Rapids: Kregel, 1998.

Melchert, Charles F. *Wise Teaching: Biblical Wisdom and Educational Ministry*. Harrisburg, Pa.: Trinity, 1998.

Stein, Robert. *The Method and Message of Jesus' Teachings*. Philadelphia: Westminster, 1978.

Wilkerson, Barbara, ed. *Multicultural Religious Education*. Birmingham, Ala.: Religious Education Press, 1997.

Zuck, Roy B. *Teaching as Jesus Taught*. Grand Rapids: Baker, 1995.

God In Us

Erickson, Millard J. *Christian Theology*. 2d ed. Grand Rapids: Baker, 1998.

González, Justo L. *Mañana: Christian Theology from a Hispanic Perspective*. Nashville: Abingdon, 1990.

LeBar, Lois E. *Education That Is Christian*. Ed. James E. Plueddemann. Wheaton: Victor, 1989.

Loder, James E. *The Logic of the Spirit: Human Development in Theological Perspective*. San Francisco: Jossey-Bass, 1998.

Loder, James E., and W. Jim Neidhardt. *The Knight's Move: The Relational Logic of the Spirit in Theology and Science*. Colorado Springs: Helmers and Howard, 1992.

Palmer, Parker J. *The Courage to Teach: Exploring the Inner Landscape of a Teacher's Life*. San Francisco: Jossey-Bass, 1998.

—————. *To Know As We Are Known: A Spirituality of Education*. San Francisco: Harper and Row, 1983.

Pazmiño, Robert W. *Basics of Teaching for Christians: Preparation, Instruction, and Evaluation*. Grand Rapids: Baker, 1998.

Westerhoff, John. *Spiritual Life: The Foundation for Preaching and Teaching*. Louisville: Westminster/John Knox, 1994.

World Council of Churches. *Spiritual Formation in Theological Education: An Invitation to Participate*. Geneva: Programme on Theological Education, World Council of Churches, 1987.

Wyckoff, D. Campbell. *The Task of Christian Education*. Philadelphia: Westminster, 1955.

God Through Us

Bosch, David J. *Transforming Mission: Paradigm Shifts in Theology of Mission*. Maryknoll, N.Y.: Orbis, 1991.

Cook, Guillermo. *The Expectation of the Poor: Latin American Base Ecclesial Communities in Protestant Perspective*. Maryknoll, N.Y.: Orbis, 1985.

Costas, Orlando E. *Liberating News: A Theology of Contextual Evangelization*. Grand Rapids: Eerdmans, 1989.

Dulles, Avery. *Models of the Church*. Exp. ed. Garden City, N.Y.: Doubleday, 1987.

Erickson, Millard J. *Christian Theology*. 2d ed. Grand Rapids: Baker, 1998.

Fackre, Gabriel. *The Christian Story: A Narrative Interpretation of Basic Christian Doctrine*. Rev. ed. Grand Rapids: Eerdmans, 1984.

Pazmiño, Robert W. *By What Authority Do We Teach? Sources for Empowering Christian Educators*. Grand Rapids: Baker, 1994.

God Beyond Us

Beaudoin, Tom. *Virtual Faith: The Irreverent Spiritual Quest of Generation X*. San Francisco: Jossey-Bass, 1998.

Harvey, Barry. *Politics of the Theological: Beyond the Piety and Power of a World Come of Age*. New York: Lang, 1995.

Lee, James M., ed. *Forging a Better Religious Education in the Third Millennium*. Birmingham, Ala.: Religious Education Press, 2000.

Loder, James E. *The Logic of the Spirit: Human Development in Theological Perspective*. San Francisco: Jossey-Bass, 1998.

Pazmiño, Robert W. *Latin American Journey: Insights for Christian Education in North America*. Cleveland: United Church Press, 1994.

Thompson, Norma, ed. *Religious Pluralism and Religious Education*. Birmingham, Ala.: Religious Education Press, 1988.

INDEX